MW00487815

Mastering the Basic Math Facts in Multiplication and Division

Strategies, Activities & Interventions to Move Students Beyond Memorization

Susan O'Connell and John SanGiovanni

HEINEMANN
Portsmouth, NH

Heinemann

361 Hanover Street

Portsmouth, NH 03801–3912

www.heinemann.com

Offices and agents throughout the world

© 2011 by Susan O'Connell and John SanGiovanni

All rights reserved. No part of this book may be reproduced in any form or by any electronic or mechanical means, including information storage and retrieval systems, without permission in writing from the publisher, except by a reviewer, who may quote brief passages in a review; and with the exception of reproducibles (identified by the *Mastering the Basic Math Facts in Multiplication and Division* copyright line), which may be photocopied for classroom use.

"Dedicated to Teachers" is a trademark of Greenwood Publishing Group, Inc.

Library of Congress Cataloging-in-Publication Data

O'Connell, Susan.

Mastering the basic math facts in multiplication and division : strategies, activities & interventions to move students beyond memorization / Susan O'Connell and John SanGiovanni.

 p. cm.

Includes bibliographical references.

ISBN-13: 978-0-325-02962-7

ISBN-10: 0-325-02962-8

1. Multiplication—Study and teaching (Elementary). 2. Division—Study and teaching (Elementary). I. SanGiovanni, John. II. Title.

QA115 .O3342011

372.7'2—dc22   2010046909

Editor: Victoria Merecki

Production: Victoria Merecki

Cover and interior designs: Palmer Creative Group

Composition: Publishers' Design and Production Services, Inc.

Manufacturing: Steve Bernier

Printed in the United States of America on acid-free paper

15 14 13 12 11 VP   2 3 4 5

Dedication

To the little guys, Colin and Liam, with love
S.O.
To Krissy, my favorite math teacher and wine connoisseur
J.S.

Contents

Foreword

Being able to add and subtract within 20 and multiply and divide within 100 is essential during the early years of schooling, and the basic facts of addition/subtraction and multiplication/division are a critical baseline, not only then but also during later work with fractions, decimals, ratio, proportion, and more. Foundational? You better believe it. Essential? Absolutely.

That said, the basic facts are also problematic. The goal is for most students to know, fluently, and with automaticity, the addition/subtraction facts, typically by the end of second grade and the multiplication/division facts, typically by the end of third grade. But far too many teachers are unable to help their students reach these goals. "Not this year," they may mutter, or, "Not all my students," or worse, "Not ever." Why is fluency with the basic facts such a challenge for so many students? In our digit-conscious culture students can spout off multiple phone and pin numbers, but not the product of 6×7! I meet and work with middle school students who are still wondering about 8×7 or $48 \div 6$ and other basic facts. Why do far too many students fail to realize that the commutative property means that $9 + 7$ and $7 + 9$ get you to the same place, 16? This drives us all crazy! Have we neglected the basics? Is this about just having students memorize the facts? No, and no!

Over twenty years ago the *Curriculum and Evaluation Standards for School Mathematics* noted that "children should master the basic facts of arithmetic that are essential components of fluency with paper-pencil and mental computation and with estimation" (47).[1] The National Research Council's *Adding It Up* dedicates almost ten pages to synthesizing the research dealing with basic fact acquisition.[2] More recently, the *Final Report of the National Mathematics Advisory Panel* points out that computational proficiency with whole number operations depends on the practice (I prefer the term *rehearsal*) necessary to develop automatic recall of addition/subtraction and multiplication/division facts.[3] Nurturing computational facility in elementary school requires that students be fluent with the basic facts of arithmetic. How do we get this done?

Over the years teachers have tried and continue to use a myriad of practice activities—oral and written exercises, games, and classroom and homework

---

[1] National Council of Teachers of Mathematics. 1989. *Curriculum and Evaluation Standards for School Mathematics.* Reston, VA: National Council of Teachers of Mathematics.

[2] National Research Council. 2001. *Adding It Up: Helping Children Learn Mathematics.* Washington, DC: National Academy Press.

[3] National Mathematics Advisory Panel. 2008. *Foundations for Success: The Final Report of the National Mathematics Advisory Panel.* Washington, DC: U.S. Department of Education.

assignments, many of them now via the Internet. At last we have a more effective option—Susan O'Connell and John SanGiovanni's *Mastering the Basic Facts in Addition and Subtraction: Strategies, Activities & Interventions to Move Students Beyond Memorization* and *Mastering the Basic Facts in Multiplication and Division: Strategies, Activities & Interventions to Move Students Beyond Memorization*. What a find!

Based on Thornton's pioneering work[4] emphasizing how thinking strategies facilitate fact acquisition, both books present activities that develop facility with the basic facts by building a conceptual understanding of the operations; following a teaching sequence designed to develop a sense of number using fact strategies and the commutative property; and using representational models and context-based problem solving. (The activities that link facts to their conceptual representations are also powerful diagnostic tools.) But there's more—related children's literature, partner activities, a professional-learning-community study guide. All these components add up to resources that engage students, from beginning activities that promote an understanding of arithmetic concepts, through fluency with the basic facts.

One final consideration: these books will be very helpful to teachers whose students' mathematical knowledge require some level of intervention. The powerful instructional opportunities these books provide not only make sense but also meet one of the key recommendations of the What Works Clearinghouse's Practice Guide *Assisting Students Struggling with Mathematics*.[5]

These books won't end up on a shelf at the back of your room. (And if you are a third/fourth-grade teacher you will probably need both of them.) You'll use them every day. You'll carry them home with you and talk about them in the faculty lounge. Just as the basic facts are "must haves" on the path to computational fluency, these books are "must haves" to help you navigate the route.

Francis (Skip) Fennell
L. Stanley Bowlsbey Professor of Education & Graduate and Professional Studies
McDaniel College, Westminster, MD
Past President, National Council of Teachers of Mathematics
Project Director, Elementary Mathematics Specialists and Teacher Leaders Project
http://mathspecialists.org

---

4 Thornton, C.A. 1978. "Emphasizing Thinking Strategies in Basic Fact Instruction." *Journal for Research in Mathematics Education*. 16: 337–355.

5 Gersten et al. 2009. *Assisting Students Struggling with Mathematics: Response to Intervention (RtI) for Elementary and Middle Schools*. Washington, DC: Institute of Education Sciences.

Acknowledgments

Many thanks to the students whose conversations about math facts inspired and excited us as we worked on this manuscript. Thanks to the following students who contributed work samples or allowed their photographs to appear within this book: Stephen Alam, Chiagozie Anyanwu, Yomi Bashorum, Joshua Baumbgardner, Julia Bonner, Cameron Brickner, Jack Cartee, Austin Cestone, Ryan Davis, Amilli Diaz, Nolan Dyer, Gabrielle Eng, Ricky Fedorchak, Brianna Galt, Jaylin Harding, Maura Hill, Yevin Hong, Colby Jardim, Caitlyn Kealy, Amira Kim, Andrew Kim, Rachel Kim, Sumin Kim, Jillian Lach, Erin Ko, Lanae Martin, Samantha Miller, Cortez Mora, Daisheau Morris, Maria Mulroe, Stephanie Owens, Arwin Pare, Keyonna Paul, Chris Perez, Alli Polinsky, Nittin Raj, Elizabeth Raney, David Rucker, Oscar Schoenfelder, Deryn Schoenfelder, Alyssa Souder, Nick Stitely, Ryan Tracey, Caroline Underwood, Grace Underwood, Emma Vittori, Paul Weatherholtz, and Michaela Wesley. It was a pleasure watching them investigate math facts.

We appreciate the collaboration of colleagues in gathering materials for this book, in particular the following teachers, math coaches, principals, and supervisors who welcomed us into their classrooms, provided insights from their own teaching, or allowed us to listen to the ideas of their students: Randi Blue, Robin Balimtas, Leslie Brickner, Shannon Callihan, Sue Donaldson, Heather Dyer, Julie Eugenio, Carol Hahn, Asha Johnson, Pamela Jones, Sally Kingsley, Olga Lloyde, Sorsha Mulroe, Kathleen Nagle, Dana Polan, Kay Sammons, and Jennifer Zin.

We are grateful to Victoria Merecki, our Heinemann editor, for her guidance from start to finish on this project. In addition, we thank Emily Birch for her vision for this book. Her discussions in the early stages of the book were invaluable.

Special thanks to our families for their patience and understanding during the writing of this book. To Sue's husband Pat, and her children Brendan and Katie, and to John's wife Kristen, and Oscar and Deryn, our warmest thanks for your continued support.

Introduction

As math teachers, we want our students to develop a quick recall of single-digit addition, subtraction, multiplication, and division facts. We label them *basic* math facts because they provide a foundation for math success. We expect that all students will master these basic skills, but that is not a simple goal to achieve. We watch some students effortlessly remember the facts and others struggle with the very same task. And we labor to find just the right strategies and activities to help all students succeed.

As teachers, we are constantly reminded that our students learn in a variety of ways. Although some students have very strong memory skills, others struggle to remember simple facts. Although some students make sense of math concepts on their own, others struggle to connect meaning to simple expressions like 3 × 5. Although some students intuitively use their knowledge of one math fact to solve a related fact, others simply get frustrated and discouraged when they cannot remember a specific sum or product. Our students are so different, and yet our goal for each of them is the same: to master basic math facts so they have a strong foundation for more complex math skills and procedures. The goal of this book is to explore numerous strategies and activities that support all students in understanding basic multiplication and division facts and committing those facts to memory. Whether you are introducing students to basic math facts, reviewing previously taught facts, or providing interventions for students who continue to struggle, this book supplies you with instructional considerations, practical strategies, and numerous classroom-tested activities.

What are basic math facts?

For the purpose of this book, basic facts are considered to be facts with factors of 0–10. In some programs, facts with single-digit factors (0–9) are considered basic, but because of the significance of the ×10 facts, they are included within this book. An understanding of ×10 facts provides an important benchmark for understanding ×5 facts or might suggest a strategy for determining ×9 facts. The inclusion of ×10 facts is based on providing a solid understanding of numbers as the foundation for our study of basic facts.

What constitutes *mastery* of basic math facts?

In the past, much of mathematics was taught in a drill and practice style. Students were simply asked to memorize their math facts, often without much attention to conceptual understanding. Through worksheets filled with single-digit computations or lengthy flash card sessions, students were asked to memorize multiplication and division facts. Our goal in today's math classrooms has shifted from memorizing facts and procedures to increased understanding of math skills and concepts. We want our students to be able to do mathematics, but we also want them to understand the math they are doing. We recognize that as math tasks increase in complexity, an understanding of facts, formulas, and algorithms will help them experience continued success. We have not changed our view of the importance of basic math facts. We know that they are a foundational skill and that without that skill our students will view even simple math tasks as daunting. We have simply expanded our expectations to include understanding as an important component of our teaching of basic math facts. So, what do we expect of our students? Our goal is both automaticity and understanding. Automaticity is students' ability to effortlessly recall a fact. If students are automatic, they have successfully committed the facts to memory. In addition, we want our students to understand, not simply remember, these important math facts.

Why memorize math facts?

Ask math teachers what they would like their students to know and be able to do, and the recall of basic math facts will undoubtedly rank high on most of their wish lists. Teachers recognize that once their students know 3×5, those students are better able to explore 3×50 or 3×55. Teachers recognize that students will have an easier time finding the solution to $3 \times \$5.00$ or $3 \times .5$. These teachers know that their students will be more successful when they are challenged with $\frac{2}{3} \times \frac{1}{5}$. As math tasks become more complex, we want our students to possess the foundational skills to be successful.

We have gained insights from brain research about demands on the working brain. As students begin to learn math facts, their brains are focused on those basic computations, but as students become automatic with basic facts, their brains are then able to focus on other aspects of the task like the challenges of place value, decimals, or fractions. Being automatic with basic facts frees the brain to focus on other math processes.

Committing basic math facts to memory speeds up math tasks. As math tasks increase in complexity, they often require multiple steps to find the solution. Multiplication with three-digit factors and division with decimals are examples of more complex computational tasks. These tasks are time-consuming, and often stressful, for students who must stop to figure out each basic fact along the way. And stopping to determine each fact disrupts the flow of the math procedure. The National Mathematics Advisory Panel (2008) urges that students develop automatic recall of multiplication and related division facts to be prepared for the study of algebra, in which solving multistep equations is a fundamental task.

Students who have committed basic math facts to memory are able to perform critical mental math tasks. They estimate answers prior to solving problems so they are able to compare their estimates to the actual answers and determine the reasonableness of their solutions. When browsing through a grocery store, students with mental math skills can determine the approximate cost of buying 4 bags of pretzels if each bag costs about $3.00, or when counting the savings in their piggy banks, they can quickly determine that their 9 nickels amount to 45 cents in savings. As students determine how to fairly share 36 cookies among 9 friends, they can automatically determine the quantity each child will receive. Mastery of basic facts provides the foundation for everyday mental math tasks.

Automaticity means the quick and effortless recall of math facts. No need to count every object. No need to think about related facts. No need to extend patterns. The answer is automatically known. Although automaticity is a goal for our students, alone it is not enough. Students must first understand the facts that they are being asked to memorize.

Why is it important to understand math facts?

During the memorization process, students are supported by an understanding of what they are being asked to memorize. Memorizing a chain of nonsensical words (e.g., *sat chair red girl a in little the*) is more difficult than memorizing a sentence in which the words have a meaning (e.g., *A little girl sat in the red chair.*). Asking students to memorize dozens of number facts can be discouraging and confusing when students view them simply as pairs of numbers. The understanding that 7 × 3 represents 7 groups of 3 items aids the memorization process.

Students who rely solely on the memorization of math facts often confuse similar facts. Consider the multiplication facts 9 × 5 = 45 and 9 × 6 = 54. The products are commonly confused by students who have only memorized answers. Students often mix up the products and respond mistakenly that 9 × 5 = 54; however, for students who have explored an understanding of multiplication, 9 × 5 = 54 just doesn't make sense: 10 × 5 = 50, so how could 9 × 5 = 54? The product has to be less than 50! A focus on understanding multiplication and division facts will provide students with a firm foundation rather than simply relying on memory.

Students who simply memorize math facts miss a prime opportunity to expand their understanding of equations. Problem solving is the central focus in today's math classrooms. To be a successful problem solver, students must be able to accurately compute answers, but more than that, they must be able to figure out how to build equations that correspond to problem situations.

> **Colin was stacking books on the shelves of his brand-new bookcase. He put 7 books on each of the 4 shelves. How many books did he put on the shelves of his bookcase?**

This problem certainly requires the student to know that 4 × 7 = 28, but even before the student can use his knowledge of math facts to find the answer, he must understand how to build an equation that works with this problem.

> *There are 4 shelves and each shelf has 7 books on it. Since each shelf has the same number of books, I can multiply. 4 groups of 7 or 4 × 7 is how I find the answer!*

As we discuss the connection between the meaning of the equation and the basic math fact, we are supporting both students' computation skills as well as building a strong foundation for problem solving.

Both the *Common Core State Standards* (National Governors Association Center for Best Practices and Council of Chief State School Officers 2010) and the National Council of Teachers of Mathematics' *Principles and Standards* (2000) emphasize the importance of students understanding the concepts of multiplication and division. The *Common Core State Standards* recommend that second graders be given opportunities to explore problems with equal-sized groups of objects to build a foundation for multiplication. Third-grade students then continue to explore the concepts, work with properties of operations, and apply their understanding of numbers and properties to develop effective strategies for multiplying and dividing. Understanding is developed first, with practice for fluency coming later.

How can we help students master basic math facts?

We expect that our students will quickly recall facts without the need for manipulatives or number strategies. Although memorization is a part of the process, we recognize that students benefit from varied opportunities to explore basic math facts before being asked to memorize them. An instructional approach in which students investigate the meaning of facts through hands-on activities and thoughtful discussions, explore strategies to support their understanding of numbers, and then engage in strategic practice to memorize the facts provides students with a strong and balanced foundation for mastery.

Understanding operations is fundamental to understanding math facts. Students develop deeper understanding of operations through problem posing, hands-on explorations, real-world examples, classroom discussions, and exploring situations from children's literature. Division scenarios that show fair sharing and multiplication stories that demonstrate combining equal groups help students strengthen their understanding of operations, and students who understand operations will find that math facts make sense.

There are many ways that students might arrive at an answer to a math fact. When multiplying 4×3, Bailey might count every object in the 4 groups of 3 to find the total, and Liam might simply remember that $4 \times 3 = 12$. Math fact strategies lie somewhere between counting each object and simply memorizing the answer. They are predictable and efficient ways to find answers. Allison knows that $3 \times 4 = 12$, so $4 \times 3 = 12$, too. Brendan might recognize doubles—if $2 \times 3 = 6$, then 4×3 is twice that amount or 12—and Katie knows that $3 \times 3 = 9$, which is 3 groups of 3, so 4×3 is just 1 more group of 3, which means 12. Strategies help students find an answer even if they forget what was memorized. Discussing math fact strategies focuses attention on number sense, operations, patterns, properties, and other critical number concepts. These big ideas related to numbers provide a strong foundation for the strategic reasoning that supports mastering basic math facts. For multiplication and division, strategic reasoning related to doubling and halving, the commutative property, zero and ones properties, recognizing patterns, and breaking numbers apart to find related products provides students with a solid foundation for mastery of math facts.

Once an understanding of operations has been developed and students have explored strategic reasoning to find solutions to basic math facts, it is time to engage students in meaningful practice so they can commit the facts to memory. Rather than long practice sessions (Remember the lengthy flash card drills of days past?), consider activities that are short in duration but easy to implement, so students are frequently engaged in valuable practice. Scattered practice—five to ten minutes a day, spread throughout the school year—yields great results. And varying the practice activities so students remain motivated and engaged is essential to the process. Brief, frequent, interactive activities that provide students with repeated exposure to math facts support automaticity.

Because of the anxiety associated with memorization tasks for many students, the practice tasks in this book do not focus on speed or elimination. Although speed drills or elimination games may be enjoyed by some students, these types of activities often intensify the frustration and anxiety of others. Students who struggle with rote memory tasks, those students who are the reason we include math fact activities in our daily schedule, are just the ones who become discouraged by the speed drills or experience humiliation when they are the first to be eliminated. These are the students we want to motivate—the students we need to engage in repeated practice sessions. You will find that many practice activities are presented throughout this book. It is important to select the ones that work for your students. Although some students find competitive activities fun and motivating, others thrive on collegial tasks.

How can this book help you?

This book is a practical guide for helping students master multiplication and division facts. It includes insights into the teaching of basic math facts including a multitude of instructional strategies, teacher tips, and classroom activities designed to help students master their facts. The emphasis is on strengthening students' understanding of numbers, patterns, and properties as an essential component of math fact teaching. Whether you are introducing your students to basic math facts, providing reviews to support their mastery, or looking for intervention strategies for students who have been exposed to math facts but have not reached mastery, this book will provide you with valuable resources, insights, and options.

You will find activities and resources for introducing students to basic math facts. You will find tips for generating student talk about math facts including examples of questions and prompts that direct students' thinking toward big ideas and lead them to insights that will simplify the task of mastering the facts. You will find activities to support varied levels of learners so that you can choose the right activity to extend learning for high-level students or modify skills to support struggling students. You will find strategies that are hands-on, engaging, and interactive to motivate reluctant students. You will find activities perfect for small-group interventions and others that work well for whole-class instruction or individual support. And you will find a CD filled with resources to ease your planning and preparation.

This book is a compilation of strategies and activities that are organized to provide a solid math facts program; however, the individual activities and strategies can be easily integrated into your existing math program to provide you with additional resources and varied instructional approaches. You may read the book from start to finish or you may focus on specific sections that address your needs. Consider your students and select the strategies and activities to match their needs, interests, learning styles, and abilities.

How is this book organized?

Throughout the following chapters, multiple teaching strategies and activities are shared to build students' understanding and automaticity with math facts. Each chapter is organized to develop essential understanding and provide a menu of possible activities for instruction, practice, and assessment. Following are highlights of the key elements in Chapters 2 through 12.

Making Connections and Focusing on the Big Ideas

Each chapter begins by connecting the new fact set to students' previous experiences and provides a brief overview of big ideas that play a key role in students' understanding of the facts and students' development of strategies related to the facts.

Developing Understanding

Each chapter provides two introductory lessons that focus on developing conceptual understanding of the highlighted math facts. One lesson is a Literature Link, introducing the facts through a story context. The other lesson, Exploring the Facts, provides a language-based and/or hands-on exploration with the new set of facts. The activities in this book employ varied instructional techniques, including the use of manipulatives, visuals, literature, and discussions, ensuring that students experience multiplication and division facts in diverse ways and that each student will be likely to experience these facts in a way that makes sense to him.

In Supporting All Learners, you will find more ideas for those students who may need additional or different types of experiences to develop understanding of the targeted facts. These activities might be done with the whole class but may also be perfect for small teacher-led groups of students. For some sets of facts, you may choose to use several of these activities; at other times, your students may not need the additional exposure. These activities simply provide you with more and varied possibilities for developing understanding.

Building Automaticity

This section focuses on building students' fluency and is broken into two parts: Targeted Practice and Monitoring Progress. In Targeted Practice, a variety of activities are shared that provide practice for that specific set of math facts. Students will have fun rolling number cubes, spinning spinners, and pulling number cards from a deck as they engage in ongoing practice through interactive activities. It is through repeated and targeted practice that students gain fluency with math facts. Templates for these activities can be found on the accompanying CD.

Along with repeated practice to gain fluency with math facts, students need constant monitoring to ensure that they are progressing in their mastery of facts. Monitoring Progress provides ideas for monitoring students' growth toward automaticity including ideas for conducting frequent Fact Checks and suggestions for varied ways to track students' progress including student conferences, progress graphs, and individual goal setting.

Connecting to Division

Multiplication facts are the primary emphasis throughout this book because of our focus on building math fact fluency. When posed with a division math fact, the most efficient way to solve it is by knowing the related multiplication fact. When the recall of multiplication facts is automatic and students understand the connection between multiplication and division facts, their fluency with division facts naturally increases.

Lessons to develop students' understanding of related division facts are included in each chapter. In addition, you will find suggestions throughout the book of activities to build division fact fluency. To attain fluency with division facts, students need ongoing opportunities to explore their connections to multiplication facts.

What is the teaching sequence of math facts within this book?

Although the chapters are organized by specific math facts (e.g., multiplying by fives), you will notice that the focus of each chapter is the big ideas that guide students to understand that set of multiplication and division facts, to create effective math strategies related to the facts, and to ultimately commit those facts to memory. This book is not simply a collection of activities; it is intended to highlight big ideas that provide a perfect focus for math facts instruction, to broaden your repertoire of instructional strategies, to provide you with dozens of easy-to-implement activity ideas, and to stimulate your reflection related to the teaching of math facts. In reviewing the organization of this book, you may also notice that the multiplication facts do not appear in numerical order (0–10), but rather appear in a sequence that focuses on the complexity of the number concepts and carefully links each new set of facts to previously explored facts, building upon students' prior knowledge.

The teaching sequence of facts suggested within this book begins with simpler facts and then connects each new set of facts to the previously mastered ones. A traditional sequence of learning math facts from 0 to 10 does not capitalize on students' prior knowledge, nor does it present simpler facts first. Beginning with ×2, ×10, and ×5 facts allows students to explore multiplication with patterns that are familiar. ×1 and ×0 facts are addressed next. Although these facts are simple to memorize, they are a bit atypical of the grouping element of multiplication (i.e., What is a group of 1? What is 0 groups of 4?). Once 0, 1, 2, 5, and 10 are mastered, students have developed a strong foundation on which to build mastery of the remaining facts.

Figure 1 outlines a brief rationale for the sequence in which the facts are introduced within this book. We recognize, however, that students and instructional programs differ and that teachers might choose, or be required, to introduce facts in a different sequence. Although we believe that there is strong justification for this sequence, we have carefully developed strategies and activities that support instruction of math facts even if the order in which you present the facts differs from the sequence described in Figure 1.

Foundation Facts	
×2	Students have extensive experience skip-counting by twos and grouping in twos (pairs) and have developed an understanding of doubling. This set of facts is a natural place to begin exploring multiplication facts.
×10	The understanding of 10 is foundational in our number system. Students have experience skip-counting by 10, grouping in tens, and working with models of 10, such as ten-frames and base-ten blocks.
×5	Students have extensive experience skip-counting by 5. They recognize connections with money concepts (nickels). Previous exploration with ×10 facts leads to the insight that multiplying by 5 can be thought of as half of multiplying by 10.
×1	Although ×1 facts are simple to memorize, we do not begin with ×1 facts because of the confusion with the grouping aspect of multiplication (e.g., groups of 1?). Providing students with opportunities to explore groups of 2, 5, and 10 provides a stronger foundation for understanding multiplication facts.
×0	×0 facts are easy for students to commit to memory because the product is always 0, but this set of facts can be challenging for concrete thinkers. It is difficult to conceptualize a group of nothing. Once students have explored multiplication with 2, 10, 5, and 1, this set of facts becomes easier to understand.
Building on the Foundation	
×3	Multiplying by 3 can be thought of as multiplying by 2 and then adding 1 more group, or as tripling a number.
×4	Multiplying by 4 can be thought of as doubling a double. The previous mastery of ×2 facts allows students to double ×2 products to find the ×4 products.
×6	Multiplying by 6 can be thought of as doubling a multiple of 3. Previous mastery of ×3 facts allows students to see that 4×6 can be thought of as double 4×3, or $(4 \times 3) + (4 \times 3)$. Previous mastery of ×5 facts also supports students with ×6 facts, knowing that the product of a ×6 fact is simply 1 set more than the product of the related ×5 fact (e.g., the product of 6×8 is 8 more than the product of 5×8).
×9	Building on knowledge of ×10 facts, the product of a ×9 fact is 1 group less than the product of the same ×10 fact (e.g., $10 \times 5 = 50$, so $9 \times 5 = 45$, which is 5 less, or $10 \times 7 = 70$ and $9 \times 7 = 63$, which is 7 less).
×8	Multiplying by 8 results in a product that is double that of multiplying by 4. With the teaching sequence suggested in this book, only two of these facts have not been explored through a different strategy (7×8 and 8×8).
×7	Multiplying by 7 may be the most difficult for students. Students can break apart the 7 (distributive property) to find that it is the sum of 5 times the factor and 2 times the factor (e.g., 7×4 is $(5 \times 4) + (2 \times 4)$). Although this works, it is more efficient to simply think *commutative property* and reverse the order of the factors. By doing this, students realize that they already know all of the ×7 facts except 7×7.

Figure 1. *This suggested teaching sequence begins with simpler facts and then connects each new set of facts to students' previous experiences.*

The lessons and activities in this book focus on strengthening students' number concepts to support their mastery of basic math facts. Teachers who have a deep understanding of big ideas related to numbers and the ways in which those big ideas relate to the teaching of math facts, and who have developed a repertoire of instructional techniques and classroom activities to highlight those big ideas, are able to simplify the task of mastering basic math facts for their students.

Why are activities and resources on a CD?

Along with the many easy-to-implement student activities within the book, you will find a teacher-friendly CD filled with customizable activities, templates, and recording sheets. Because the CD activities are Microsoft Word documents rather than permanent PDF files, you can easily modify the activity page to make it simpler or more complex, personalize the tasks to motivate and engage your students, and adapt the activities to maintain your students' interest. A resource presented in one chapter to provide practice with a specific set of facts has often been modified for other fact sets (see Additional Resources on the CD) to provide you with a wide array of practice options. The CD also includes teacher tools (e.g., hundred charts, multiplication tables, game templates, assessment options) to simplify your planning and reduce your preparation time.

Resource for Professional Learning Communities

Effective teachers constantly reflect on their own teaching. They gather new ideas, try them with students, reflect on their successes, and find ways to continually refine their teaching. At the conclusion of this book, questions are posed to stimulate reflection about the key points within the chapters. These guiding questions are designed for your personal reflection or for use in school-based study groups. Discussion about math facts instruction within our professional learning communities broadens our understanding and improves our teaching.

Our Goal

The purpose of this book is to explore ways to support all students in mastering multiplication and division facts. By focusing on big ideas, strengthening students' understanding of math operations, developing strategic thinking, and providing varied and engaging practice tasks to promote fluency, our students will be better equipped to both understand math facts and commit the facts to memory. Whether you are introducing students to basic facts, reviewing facts, or providing remediation for struggling students, this book will provide you with insights and activities to simplify this complex, but critical, component of math teaching.

CHAPTER ONE

Understanding Multiplication and Division

It is essential that students build an understanding of the concepts of multiplication and division prior to memorizing multiplication and division facts. Students who understand the concepts of multiplication and division recognize the connection between math facts and real situations (i.e., 2 vases of flowers with 9 flowers in each vase would be represented by 2×9). These students are better equipped to effectively solve math problems by choosing the operation that makes sense

(i.e., "Both vases have the same number of flowers, so we just multiply by 2 to find the total."). They are better able to make reasonable judgments about products and quotients (i.e., "2 × 9 can't be 11 because you have 2 groups of 9 flowers. That just wouldn't make sense!"). And students who understand the concepts of multiplication and division are better prepared to begin the task of memorizing math facts because they understand what they are being asked to memorize.

Exploring Big Ideas to Develop Math Fact Strategies

Big ideas are essential to the development of understanding (Wiggins and McTighe 1998; Fosnot and Dolk 2001). It is the big ideas about numbers that help students make sense of math facts and form the foundation for their development of math fact strategies. The following big ideas are central to the teaching of multiplication and division facts.

Our number system is a system of patterns.

Once students understand that our number system is a system of patterns, they begin to recognize patterns in math facts that will help them make sense of, and remember, the facts (Fuson 2003). Noticing that the products of ×6 facts are twice the product of ×3 facts, or that the product of ×5 facts have a 5 or 0 in the ones place, will lead to some interesting discussions as students attempt to explain these observations. Because our number system is a system of patterns, patterns emerge throughout the exploration of multiplication and division facts. These patterns make math facts predictable.

Numbers can count objects or groups.

From their experiences with counting, addition, and subtraction, students have developed an understanding that *2* represents two objects and *6* represents six objects, and these objects can be counted, combined, or compared. When transitioning to multiplication, the numbers in the expression no longer represent individual objects. One number represents the number of groups or sets, and the other number represents the size of each group or set. Students begin to understand unitizing—that numbers can represent a group or unit. Without this understanding, multiplication products make no sense. 2 + 3 and 2 × 3 do not result in the same total. It is the symbol that tells us that in the addition expression, we simply combine 2 quantities to find the sum, but in the multiplication expression, we are considering 2 groups of 3 objects.

The order of the factors does not change the product (the commutative property).

Whether students are visualizing 2 groups of a certain size (e.g., 2 × 5 or 2 groups of 5) or whether they are visualizing groups of 2 (e.g., 5 × 2 or 5 groups of 2), they begin to notice that the products are the same. Investigations will confirm the commutative (order) property, and when students' experiences convince them that the order of the factors will not change the sum, the task of memorizing math facts is immediately simplified through the realization that they need only memorize half as many facts (i.e., if they know the product of 2 × 5, then they also know the product of 5 × 2).

Addition and multiplication are related operations.

There is a connection between the operations of addition and multiplication. Both operations focus on the process of combining parts to find totals, but multiplication provides a mathematical shortcut to the process when the groups are equal. Multiplication is often referred to as *repeated addition* because of this connection. In the same way, subtraction and division are related operations and division can be thought of as repeated subtraction.

Multiplication and division are inverse operations.

There is a connection between the operations of multiplication and division. If we know the number of groups and the size of each group, we can determine the whole (multiplication). If we know the whole and the size of each group, we can determine the number of groups (quotative division). If we know the whole and the number of groups, we can determine the size of each group (partitive division). Fact families are often explored to highlight this connection (e.g., 5 × 4 = 20; 4 × 5 = 20; 20 ÷ 5 = 4; 20 ÷ 4 = 5).

Numbers are flexible.

Numbers can be broken apart in varied ways. In the expression 4 × 6, 6 might be broken into 2 threes, so 4 × 6 is the same as 4(3 + 3), which is the same as (4 × 3) + (4 × 3). Or we could split the 6 into 1 + 5, so 4 × 6 is the same as 4(1 + 5), which is the same as (4 × 1) + (4 × 5). The distributive property is the foundation for the understanding that splitting large factors and then finding the sum of the two products is a way to find unknown products.

These big ideas about numbers are central to students' understanding and should guide the types of questions that are posed during student explorations or class discussions.

What do the numbers in this equation represent? How do you know that?

What patterns did you notice in the factors and products?

Does the order of the factors affect the product? Give examples to justify your thinking.

Can you write an addition equation to match this multiplication equation? How do you know that they represent the same thing?

Do you notice a connection between this multiplication equation and this division equation? Explain.

Can you break apart one of the factors to help you find the product?

Our goal is to continually reinforce the big ideas related to math facts as we help students develop multiplication strategies.

Introducing the Concepts of Multiplication and Division

Initial experiences with multiplication and division are designed to help students understand the mathematical processes, as well as their symbolic representations. Guided investigations help students gain new insights about ways to solve and represent multiplication and division problems, and hands-on experiences and thoughtful discussions generate excitement and help students grasp the new concepts.

Investigating the Concept of Multiplication: Comparing Methods for Solving Problems

Begin a guided investigation to explore the concept of multiplication by filling 5 party favor bags with 3 stickers in each bag. Show students the 5 party bags and pose the following class problem:

> It's Bailey's birthday! She made a favor bag for each of the 5 guests at her birthday party. She put 3 stickers in each bag. How many stickers were in the bags altogether?

Ask students to work in pairs to find the answer. Give each pair some counters and a paper to record or draw their ideas. After students have had time to explore the problem, begin a class discussion to share their solutions. Ask students to report how many stickers they believe are in the bags and to explain how they found their answers. Some typical strategies might include:

- placing the counters in groups of 3 until there are 5 groups and then counting them to get the total of 15

- adding 3 + 3 + 3 + 3 + 3 = 15, or adding 3 + 3 = 6, then 6 + 3 = 9, then 9 + 3 = 12, then 12 + 3 = 15

- arranging their counters into 5 piles with 3 in each pile and then skip-counting to get to 15

Talk as you record their ideas on the board. Record an addition equation to represent the problem: *3 + 3 + 3 + 3 + 3 = 15*. Record a grouping statement to represent the problem: *5 groups of 3 = 15*. After you have recorded students' ideas, record the multiplication equation: *5 × 3 = 15*. Compare the statement "5 groups of 3 = 15" to the equation 5 × 3 = 15. Talk about the new way of recording the process using the multiplication symbol. Discuss what each number in the equation represents. Then, confirm students' solutions by opening the party bags to find the total number of stickers in the 5 bags. Confirm that all of their methods would lead to the answer and that multiplication, like counting, skip-counting, or adding equal groups, is another way to find the solution.

Pose another problem for pairs to solve using counters, pictures, or another strategy of their choice. Modify the data to make the problems easier or more challenging for students who might benefit from a modification. Some possible problems:

> Mrs. King took 6 boxes of crayons out of her desk. There were 5 crayons in each box. How many crayons were there altogether?

> Molly's bookcase had 8 shelves. There were 6 books on each shelf. How many books did she have?

Talk about solutions with the class (or with small groups of students if you have varied the problems for different groups). Record students' methods for finding the answer. Be sure to record the addition equation (e.g., *5 + 5 + 5 + 5 + 5 + 5 = 30*), a grouping statement (e.g., *6 groups of 5 = 30*), and the related multiplication equation (e.g., *6 × 5 = 30*) and to make connections between these different ways of representing students' methods.

Repeated Practice with the Concept: How Many Fish?

Provide students with multiple opportunities to practice representing and solving multiplication problems. Exploring the concept through varied problems and interactive activities allows students to generalize the concept and become more comfortable with the numeric representations.

In this investigation, students work with partners and use number cards to generate a specific number of fishbowls and the quantity of fish to place in each bowl. The goal is to find the total number of fish in all of their bowls. Each pair of students is given 5 fishbowl templates (see template on CD) and a set of at least 50 counters, or goldfish crackers, to represent fish, as well as a large paper to record their solutions. Each pair will also need 2 sets of number cards, a set of 1–5 cards and a set of 1–10 cards (see CD). Students pick a card from the 1–5 deck to indicate the number of fishbowls they will have, and place that number of bowls in front of them. Next, students pick a card from the 1–10 deck to indicate the number of fish that will be in each bowl. Partners, like those in Figure 1.1, work together to determine the total number

Tip **Connecting Concrete and Pictorial to Abstract**

Although using manipulatives and drawing pictures help students conceptualize the multiplication or division process, be sure to record the equations to bridge the concrete and pictorial methods to the abstract representation.

Figure 1.1 *Students first use manipulatives and then draw and write equations to represent the total number of fish in their bowls.*

of fish. When they have found a solution, they record it on their paper with drawings and the multiplication equation. Sharing their drawings during a circle time discussion will allow students to see different ways to draw the scenario and to talk about their strategies. Focus attention on their representations (drawings and equations). Remind students that in mathematics, drawings are symbolic, so a circle might represent a fishbowl and an *X* might represent a fish.

Exploring Symbolic Representations Understanding the big idea that equations are simply symbolic representations of situations is a foundational understanding. In a multiplication equation, one factor represents the number of groups or sets and the other factor represents the size of each group or set. This is a huge shift from students' previous understanding of equations when working with the operations of addition and subtraction in which each number in the equation represents a quantity and the quantities are combined or compared. $2 + 5$ and 2×5 are very different expressions, and students benefit from classroom experiences that help them make sense of that difference (see Figure 1.2).

Repeatedly recording the expression (e.g., 3×4) or equation (e.g., $3 \times 4 = 12$) connects the symbolic representation to the concept of multiplication. Ask probing questions to focus students on the meaning of the numbers in equations.

What does the 3 represent?

What does the 4 represent?

How is that different from 3 + 4?

Which is greater: 3 × 4 or 3 + 4? Why?

Note that students sometimes confuse the number representing how many groups with the number representing the size of each group (e.g., in 3×4, 3 represents the number of groups and 4 represents the size of the group). Attempt to clarify this by frequently verbalizing that 3×4 is 3 *groups of* 4. However, it is most important that students recognize that the numbers represent two different things (number of groups and size of group) or the product does not make sense. The commutative property reminds us that order will not matter when moving toward automaticity with math facts.

Figure 1.2 *This student demonstrates his ability to create accurate addition and multiplication equations about the legs on 2 spiders.*

$$8 + 8 = 16 \qquad\qquad 2 \times 8 = 16$$

Spiders have 8 legs.

Exploring Division

Once students have had opportunities to explore the concept of multiplication, provide problems that develop the concept of division. In our earlier multiplication investigation, students were asked to find the total number of crayons when Mrs. King had 6 boxes with 5 crayons in each box. Pose the following division problem.

> Mrs. King had 30 crayons. There were 5 in each box. How many boxes did she have?

Have students use manipulatives, draw pictures, and ultimately write division equations for the problem. Remember that division can be thought of as partitive or quotative. *How many boxes* of crayons is asking for the number of groups (quotative). The problem might also be:

> Mrs. King had 6 boxes of crayons. There were 30 crayons altogether. How many crayons were in each box?

This problem is asking for the *number in each box* and is an example of partitive division. It is helpful to explore both types of division through problems, hands-on explorations, and lots of discussion.

Tip A division expression can represent two questions:

How many in each group (partitive)?

How many groups (quotative)?

Using Models to Represent Multiplication and Division

Students' understanding is deepened when they can visualize the multiplication and division processes. Often, teachers engage students in acting out multiplication or division scenarios or modeling the processes on a whiteboard, an overhead, or a document camera. We encourage students to create their own visuals for multiplication and division processes through their drawings or explorations with manipulatives. Each time students visualize the processes, they become increasingly familiar with the meanings of these operations. Multiplication Fact Boxes (see CD) challenge students to represent math facts in varied ways. Arrays, set models, area models, and number lines all create visual representations of multiplication and division and should be integrated frequently into math facts lessons.

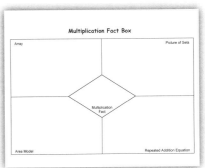

Arrays

An array shows objects in rows and columns. Real materials (e.g., raisins, buttons, beans) or manipulatives (e.g., counters, cubes, square tiles) can be arranged in rows to represent multiplication and division facts. Because arrays are made of equal rows, you can multiply to determine the total number of objects in the array. Arrays demonstrate the efficiency of multiplication. Rather than counting all of the objects or adding each row or column, students can determine the total quickly by knowing their math facts!

Rather than memorizing the commutative property, student explorations with arrays prove that the order of the factors does not affect the product. Creating an array with 4 rows of 3 buttons or an array with 3 rows of 4 buttons requires the same number of buttons (see Figure 1.3).

Tip The Common Core State Standards recommend the development of students' understanding of multiplication and division through activities involving arrays, area models, and equal-sized sets.

Figure 1.3 *Hands-on explorations convince students of the commutative property.*

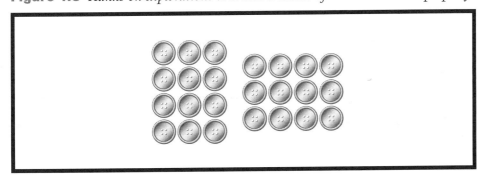

Set Models

Drawing sets is a simple way for students to visualize multiplication and division. Simply drawing a circle to represent each group and placing the appropriate number of Xs in each circle is a quick way for students to model a multiplication problem and requires no additional classroom materials. To represent a division scenario, students might draw a designated number of Xs and then circle specific size groups.

Drawing sets is an effective way to focus attention on the commutative property (see Figure 1.4). As students draw 2 sets of 5 dogs and 5 sets of 2 dogs, they begin to notice that the total number of dogs is the same despite the different groupings. Encouraging students to observe, discuss, and make conjectures based on their drawings leads them to the conclusion that the order of the factors does not affect the product.

Area Models

Shading, or outlining, rectangular regions on grid paper (see CD), and then examining the relationship between the total number of squares in the rectangular region and the number of squares along the length and width of the region, provides additional insight and is another helpful way to visualize mul-

Figure 1.4 *Explorations in drawing sets allow students to visualize the commutative property (see CD for a description of the* How Many Tallies? *activity).*

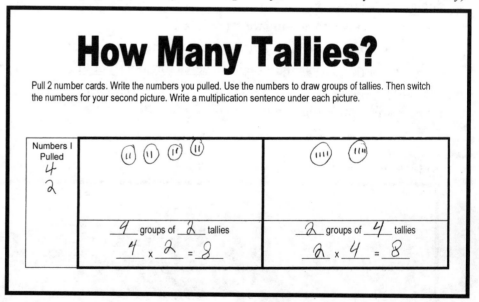

tiplication. Explore the connection with division by having students begin by counting the total number of squares in the rectangular area and then using the number of squares in the width to determine the number of squares in the length.

Area models are also effective in the development of the commutative property. Once students have highlighted the area for a multiplication fact, the rectangle can be cut out and simply rotated to represent the connected multiplication fact (see Figure 1.5).

Number Lines

A number line is a common tool to show the process of skip-counting. In skip-counting, as in multiplication, each jump is the same distance. Number lines allow students to visualize multiplication facts using the number of jumps and the size of each jump (e.g., 3×2 is 3 jumps of 2).

Double number lines (see Figure 1.6) can be used to explore the commutative property, with students showing 3 jumps of 2 on the top of the number line and 2 jumps of 3 on the bottom of the number line. In both cases, the jumps end at 6 on the number line!

Figure 1.5 *A simple rotation of an area model illustrates that the order of the factors does not change the product.*

Tip Models build understanding of the commutative property.

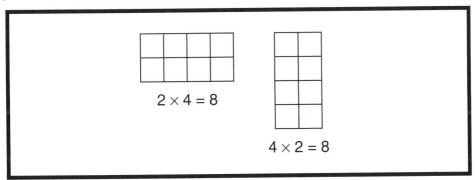

$2 \times 4 = 8$

$4 \times 2 = 8$

Figure 1.6 *Plotting math facts on a double number line allows students to gain powerful insights about the commutative property.*

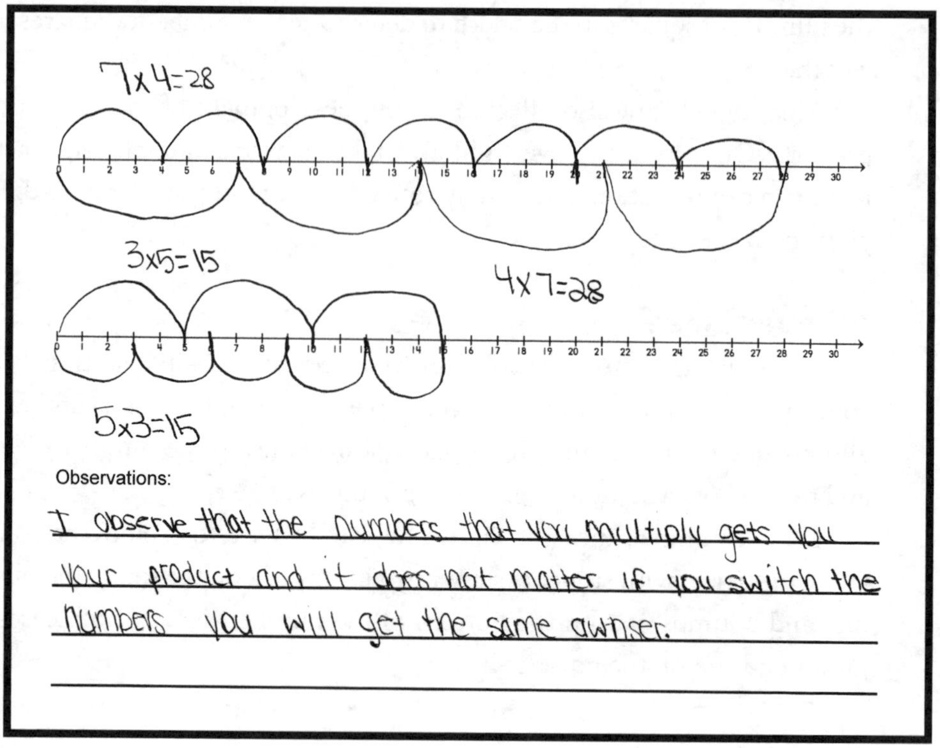

Observations:

I observe that the numbers that you multiply gets you your product and it does not matter if you switch the numbers you will get the same awnser.

Posing/Writing Problems to Develop an Understanding of Math Facts

Tip Teaching math facts through problem-solving investigations strengthens students' understanding of the facts and builds their problem-solving skills.

Posing problems to explore multiplication and division facts develops a strong connection between an equation and a mathematical situation. Throughout the book, student explorations are set in problem contexts to ensure that students are developing conceptual understanding. Real-world experiences provide engaging problem data from buying items at a grocery store (e.g., the cost of 6 bags of potato chips) to dividing food for a picnic (e.g., fairly sharing 35 strawberries among 5 children). And asking students to write their own problems for math facts provides a solid assessment of their understanding of the expressions.

Exploring Multiplication and Division Through Children's Literature

When reading and discussing the math situations in children's literature, students experience the math operations in a context that makes sense to them. In *Amanda Bean's Amazing Dream* (Neuschwander 1998), Amanda learns that multiplication can be much more efficient than counting as she tries to count the many objects in her dream. In *Stacks of Trouble* (Brenner 2000), a young boy is overwhelmed by the pile of dirty dishes that seems to multiply right before his eyes. In *The Doorbell Rang* (Hutchins 1986), children experience division as they fairly share the cookies made by their mom. Students might write their own multiplication or division problems after exploring the data in *What Comes in 2's, 3's, & 4's?* (Aker 1990) or *Each Orange Had 8 Slices* (Giganti 1999).

The following chapters contain many Literature Links that offer lesson suggestions that focus on children's literature. A resource list of all titles is located in the References. To make the most of the integration of literature into math facts lessons, a "before, during, after" approach is suggested. *Before* reading the story, set the context for the story, assess prior knowledge, or pose a question to guide students' thinking as they read or listen to the story. *During* reading, ask students to make predictions or reread the story as students act out the events using manipulatives. *After* reading, further explore the concepts through investigations, problems, and discussions. The stories engage students, set a context for further explorations, and provide a memorable lesson related to the math facts being studied.

Ongoing Reference to the Concepts As students go through the school day, there are many opportunities to reinforce the concept of multiplication and make connections between multiplication and addition and between multiplication and division. Capitalize on everyday examples of multiplication and division to provide repeated exposure to the concepts.

Students' desks are placed in groups of 4.

Students are split into teams of 5 for P.E. class.

The cafeteria places 3 carrot sticks on each student's tray.

Beginning with Understanding

Automaticity with math facts is our goal, but before any math fact fluency practice begins, understanding of the operations is essential. Through investigations, discussions, visual models, stories, and hands-on explorations, students develop an understanding of the concepts of multiplication and division and are then ready to begin to commit those facts to memory.

CHAPTER TWO

Multiplying by 2

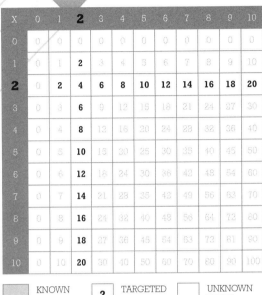

X	0	1	**2**	3	4	5	6	7	8	9	10
0	0	0	0	0	0	0	0	0	0	0	0
1	0	1	**2**	3	4	5	6	7	8	9	10
2	0	**2**	**4**	**6**	**8**	**10**	**12**	**14**	**16**	**18**	**20**
3	0	3	**6**	9	12	15	18	21	24	27	30
4	0	4	**8**	12	16	20	24	28	32	36	40
5	0	5	**10**	15	20	25	30	35	40	45	50
6	0	6	**12**	18	24	30	36	42	48	54	60
7	0	7	**14**	21	28	35	42	49	56	63	70
8	0	8	**16**	24	32	40	48	56	64	72	80
9	0	9	**18**	27	36	45	54	63	72	81	90
10	0	10	**20**	30	40	50	60	70	80	90	100

	KNOWN FACTS	**2**	TARGETED FACTS		UNKNOWN FACTS

We begin our study of math facts by focusing on 2 as a factor. Students have skip-counted by twos since their days in kindergarten. They are familiar with the concept of doubling from their work in addition. They have discussed odd and even numbers and explored the concept of pairs. Because of these previous experiences that develop fundamental understandings for multiplication and division by 2, the perfect place to begin our journey for math fact understanding and automaticity is with ×2 facts!

Focusing on the Big Ideas

Big ideas about mathematics provide the backdrop for our math facts experiences. When focusing on multiplication with 2 as a factor, the following are some big ideas.

Multiplication by 2 is the same as doubling.

Students have already explored doubling during their study of addition. Most students have successfully memorized their doubles addition facts. In multiplication, students recognize that doubling 4, or 4 + 4, can be expressed as 2 × 4, or 2 groups of 4. Once this is understood, many students will recognize that they already know their ×2 facts.

Numbers stand for a variety of things. Operation symbols help us determine what the numbers represent.

From their initial experiences with the concept of multiplication, students are beginning to see that numbers in multiplication equations represent different things than numbers in addition equations. Understanding that in the expression 2 × 6, 2 represent *two groups or sets* and 6 represents *six items in each group* (or the size of each set) is critical to students' understanding of these math facts. Without this understanding, multiplication products make no sense.

Our number system is a system of patterns.

Noticing that the products of ×2 facts are all even numbers leads to some interesting discussions as students attempt to explain this observation. After investigating, visualizing, and discussing ×2 facts, students will recognize that multiplying by 2 results in pairs, helping to explain why these products must be even numbers.

The order of the factors does not change the product (the commutative property).

Whether students are visualizing the doubling process, 2 groups of a certain size (e.g., 2 × 5 or 2 groups of 5), or whether they are visualizing groups of 2, or pairs (e.g., 5 pairs or 5 groups of 2), they will notice that the products are the same. This insight immediately simplifies the task of memorizing math facts through the realization that students need only memorize half as many facts (i.e., if they know the product of 2 × 5, then they also know the product of 5 × 2).

Key questions related to the big ideas for ×2 facts:

What does it mean to have twice as much? What does it mean to double a quantity?

What does it mean to have half as much (connection to division)?

What does the symbol in that equation tell you? Would the total be different if I changed the symbol from + to ×? Why?

What do the numbers in this equation represent?

What patterns do you notice in the products?

Does the order of the factors affect the product? Give examples to justify your thinking.

How are a sum and product alike? How are they different?

Our goal is to continually reinforce the big ideas related to math facts as we help students develop multiplication strategies.

Understanding ×2 Facts

Literature Link: *Two of Everything*

Students are better able to make sense of new ideas when those new ideas are connected to previously acquired knowledge. As we introduce multiplication with 2 as a factor, we rely on connecting this new knowledge to our students' previous understanding of doubles in addition. Recognizing that doubles can be represented with a multiplication equation as well as an addition equation is an important understanding. In the folktale *Two of Everything* by Lily Toy Hong (1993), a couple finds a magic pot that doubles everything that falls inside. The story is fun and engaging and sets a context for further discussions about the concept of doubling.

Before Reading   Prior to reading the story, posing questions similar to the following will activate students' prior knowledge, set a purpose for reading the story, and highlight some key math vocabulary (*doubling, twice*).

Have you ever wanted to have twice as much of something?

What do I mean when I say twice as much? Can you give me an example?

What does it mean to double something? Can you give me an example?

We are going to read a story about a couple who find a magic pot that doubles everything that falls inside. Would you like to have that pot? Why?

During Reading   When reading the story to students for the first time, it is important to move through the story without too many interruptions for discussion. Students are anxious to hear what will happen next, and lengthy discussions in the midst of the story can be distracting and result in students forgetting the last event that occurred in the story or simply losing interest in the story. Pause slightly during the first reading to predict events, like having students guess how many items will be pulled out of the pot at various times throughout the story. Remember that students love to hear stories, so rereading a story and having students discuss events, reenact events with manipulatives, or make connections to math equations are effectively done during a second reading or a simple retelling of story events.

After Reading   Begin a class discussion about the story. Posing questions similar to the following will stimulate students' thinking and allow you to assess their understanding of the doubling concept.

What doubled in the story? Name some of the items that doubled.

How many gold coins (or name another item) fell into the pot? How many were taken out? How did you know? Did you add? Did you just know the double?

Are doubling *and* twice as many *the same? Explain.*

Can you find twice as many by adding? How? (You might record a sample addition equation like 3 + 3 = 6.)

Can you find twice as many by multiplying? How? (You might record a sample multiplication equation like 2 × 3 = 6 and talk about 2 groups of 3 or twice 3 or double 3.)

Ask students if they would like to have that pot. Ask them to think about what they would put inside and what they would take out. Have them turn and tell their partner, but remind them to use numbers so their partner knows exactly what they would put in and take out (e.g., "I would put 5 dollars in and take 10 dollars out or I would put 6 bags of candy in and get 12 bags of candy out."). After students have shared with their partners, ask a few to share with the class. As students share ideas, record multiplication equations to go with their ideas (e.g., *2 × 5 = 10* or *2 × 6 = 12*). Begin an exploration of doubles by using yellow counters in plastic zipper bags to represent gold coins in a purse. Pose doubling problems by showing students a bag (e.g., a bag with 3 gold coins) and challenging them to turn and tell their partner the number of coins that would be taken out with twice as many bags (e.g., 6 coins). Record and verbalize the multiplication equations as students share them with the group (i.e., *2 × 3 = 6*; 2 bags with 3 coins in each bag is a total of 6 gold coins).

Place 1 to 10 yellow counters (gold coins) in plastic zipper bags and give each pair or team 3 or 4 bags containing different quantities. Have additional yellow counters available for students who need to explore the problems by actually creating the doubles. Ask the students to determine how many coins are in the bag now and how many coins they would have if the bag fell in the pot (see Figure 2.1). Ask the students to record addition and multiplication equations to show how they determined *twice as many* (see Gold Coin Doubles recording sheet on the CD).

As you move through the room, identify students who might benefit from exploring this activity in a more guided way. As you work with those students in a small teacher-led group, pose one of the following story-related problems for others to solve with partners. Have manipulatives available for those who need them. Ask students to record a multiplication equation that would solve their problem and to explain their answer (see Figure 2.2). Note the differing levels of complexity of the problems. Assign partners a task that meets their needs.

Figure 2.1 *Students work together to find the doubles of the coins in their bags.*

> Mr. Haktak wanted a special gift for his wife. He picked 6 roses from his garden and placed them in the pot. How many roses did he have to give to Mrs. Haktak? How do you know?

> Mrs. Haktak had a busy day and forgot to make dinner. She found 3 corn muffins and 4 carrots and placed them in the pot. What did she take out of the pot for dinner? How do you know?

> Mr. Haktak put 4 dimes in the pot. Mrs. Haktak put 7 nickels in the pot. Who had more money when they took their coins out of the pot? Justify your answer.

Having students write their own word problems will help you assess whether they understand the connection between the equation and the problem situation. To conclude the lesson, ask students to write a doubles problem about the magic pot and show how they would solve their problem. Have students share their word problems with the class.

Figure 2.2 *This student understands that doubling means to multiply by 2.*

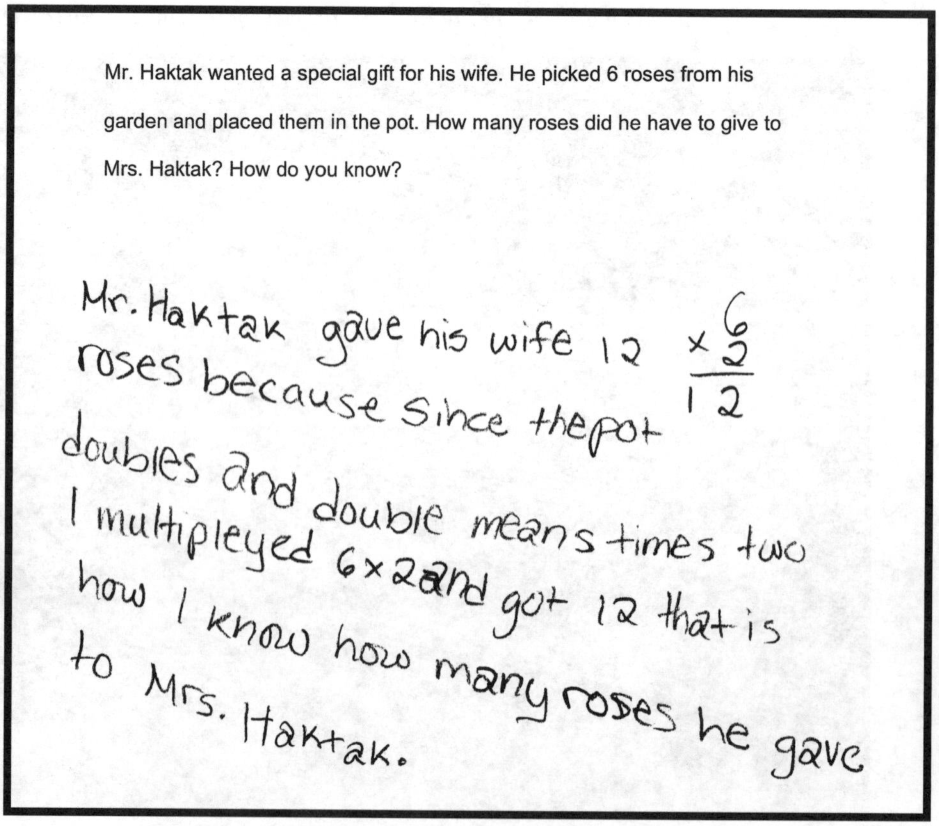

Mr. Haktak wanted a special gift for his wife. He picked 6 roses from his garden and placed them in the pot. How many roses did he have to give to Mrs. Haktak? How do you know?

Mr. Haktak gave his wife 12 roses because since the pot doubles and double means times two I multipleyed 6×2 and got 12 that is how I know how many roses he gave to Mrs. Haktak.

$$\begin{array}{r} 6 \\ \times\ 2 \\ \hline 12 \end{array}$$

Extend the lesson by placing some coin bags in your math center so that during center times, students can select bags, record the quantity in each bag, and write the multiplication and addition equations that show the double.

Exploring the Facts: A Focus on Pairs

The Literature Link explorations focus on multiplication by 2 as a doubling process (e.g., 2 groups of *n*), but another way to think about multiplication with 2 as a factor is finding the total for sets of twos, or pairs (e.g., *n* groups of 2). Posing problems, and asking students to draw pictures to represent the problems, is a great way to explore pairs. Begin by posing the following problem.

> Mrs. Short baked some yummy chocolate brownies. She placed 6 plates on the kitchen table and put 2 brownies on each plate. How many brownies did she put on plates?

Begin a think-aloud as you consider how to represent the problem. "I'm having a hard time doing this in my head. What can I do so I can see what this looks like?" Students might suggest drawing 6 circles to show the plates for the brownies. Draw the plates and continue by drawing 2 squares on each one to represent the brownies. Ask students how you can figure out how many brownies you have altogether.

- Students might suggest counting each one. Acknowledge that would work. Ask students if there might be a faster way.

- A student might suggest skip-counting by 2 to find the total, a great opportunity to acknowledge that there are pairs of brownies so skip-counting by 2 would make sense and be faster than counting them each individually.

- A student might suggest adding $2 + 2 + 2 + 2 + 2 + 2$, which would certainly give the answer because you are looking for a total number of brownies on all 6 plates, but does involve a lengthy equation.

The student in Figure 2.3 mentions multiplication as a method and shows how she found her answer by drawing and skip-counting. If students do not suggest multiplication as a possible way to find the total, the teacher might pose a question for students to consider with a partner. "Is addition the only operation that would work?" If multiplication is suggested, probe for reasoning (i.e., "Why would multiplication work? How would the equation look?").

Figure 2.3 *This student recognizes the process as multiplication, but finds her answer by drawing and skip-counting, showing her understanding of the expression 6 × 2.*

Probing to stimulate thinking and clarifying ideas to help students process the suggestions are key teacher roles. "So, you are saying that we could multiply by 2 because every plate has 2 brownies, so it would be 6 × 2 because it's 6 plates of 2 brownies?" Recording the multiplication equation while thinking aloud provides students with verbal and visual evidence of the thinking.

Repeating the process with a similar problem, but this time having students draw the picture to represent the problem and suggest the related multiplication equation, allows us to assess their understanding. Students might work with partners to solve the following problem.

> Mrs. Short placed 8 plates on the kitchen table and put 2 strawberries on each plate. How many strawberries did she put on plates?

As students work, we have the opportunity to move through the room to observe and support. Some students may be drawing pictures, and others may be simply using equations to solve the problems. For those drawing pictures, ask if they might be able to solve the problems without the pictures and how they might be able to do that. For those who are using equations, pose problems with more challenging data (e.g., 11 plates of brownies). Our observations are critical for determining those students who might benefit from additional instruction in a small teacher-led group.

Supporting All Learners

Some students quickly grasp the idea of multiplication with 2 as a factor, but others may need additional time, and different types of experiences, to develop understanding. Following are additional ×2 activities that may be perfect for small teacher-led groups.

Revisit the Story   Reread the story *Two of Everything*, having students use blocks or counters to act out the events in the story. Have the students use their counters to show what happened to the purse, hairpin, gold coins, coat, and Mr. and Mrs. Haktak after they fell into the pot. Talk about the doubles and record the multiplication equations as students explore the doubles. While you work with your small group to provide more exposure to the ideas, the remainder of the class might work in pairs on a ×2 fact game.

Observing Patterns with Twos   Recognizing patterns can support students in their understanding of multiplication facts and their ability to commit those facts to memory. Ask students to find the products for ×2 facts (see *Observing Doubles* activity on CD). Once they have completed the math facts, have them work with partners to check their answers. If partners do not agree on the products, have them raise their hands for your assistance. If they agree on the products, ask them to examine the facts, looking for any patterns they might see, and to record their observations. Once students have recorded observations, guide them in a discussion to focus on the patterns they have noticed. Observations will likely include:

Each equation has 2 as a factor.

The products were 2, 4, 6, 8 . . . or counting by twos or adding 2 to the previous product.

The products are all even numbers.

Each product is double one of the factors.

Notice how these observations relate to the big ideas discussed earlier in the chapter. Observing math facts and attempting to explain their observations provide a rich exploration into numbers and number properties and result in a better understanding of the math facts. Frequently ask questions, such as the following, to stimulate thinking.

If we switched the order of the equations would the products still form a pattern (e.g., 2 × 4 = n, 2 × 7 = n, 2 × 1 = n . . .)?

We noticed that all of the products were even numbers. Could the product be an odd number when you multiply by 2? Why?

Exploring the Commutative Property with Manipulatives As we mentioned in Chapter 1, a big idea about multiplication is that the order of the factors does not affect the product (the commutative property). Students who understand the commutative property will have an easier time memorizing products simply because they will be memorizing half as many math facts. Exploring this property with manipulatives can help students grasp this big idea. Provide students with manipulatives (e.g., colored counters or cubes). Have them determine the answers to the following questions using their manipulatives.

> Colin had 2 baskets with 3 apples in each basket. How many apples did he have?

> Colin had 3 baskets with 2 apples in each basket. How many apples did he have?

> Bailey had 2 purses with 4 coins in each purse. How many coins did she have?

> Bailey had 4 purses with 2 coins in each purse. How many coins did she have?

Discuss the problems, representing them as multiplication equations, guiding students to the insight that the order of the factors does not affect the product. Once students get it, suggesting they "think doubles" when either factor is 2 will simplify their recall of the ×2 facts.

Tip It can be easy to assume that all students understand how multiplication charts work, but some students simply don't get it. Take the time to explain the rows and columns. Provide practice in finding facts. Using strips of transparent, but lightly colored, plastic to overlay on rows and columns helps struggling students focus on the facts and more easily locate answers.

Writing a Doubles Story   Create a doubles story with the class or a small group of students. Perhaps a magician has a magic hat and everything that goes inside it doubles or a child finds a pair of magic glasses and sees double when she looks through them. Together, decide on the story idea and brainstorm a few doubles situations, recording the ideas on chart paper and labeling them with the appropriate multiplication equations. Then, have students work in pairs to write pages for a class book (see Figure 2.4). Staple the pages together to create the class doubles book and place the book in the classroom library or math center area so students can reread it.

Figure 2.4 *This page about spots on 2 dogs was added to the class multiplication book.*

Each dog has 3 spots. Double the spots. There are 6 spots.
2 × 3 = 6

Building Automaticity

After students have engaged in a variety of activities to understand multiplication with 2 as a factor, it is time to provide them with repeated opportunities to practice the facts. In targeted practice, we focus on building automaticity. This practice is short in duration on any given day but is a routine part of the daily math time.

Targeted Practice

The Value of Math Fact Games   Beyond the enjoyment, there are many benefits to incorporating games into math fact instruction. Games actively engage students in learning and challenge students to verbalize their thinking. Playing games helps students develop number sense and boosts problem-solving skills. Games offer repetition without boredom. Students play over and over and still want to keep playing! Capitalize on the benefits of math games by selecting meaningful games that target specific facts. Following are some fact games that target ×2 facts.

Rolling for Doubles   Provide each pair of students with a 1–6 number cube and a *Rolling for Doubles* recording sheet (see CD). Students take turns rolling the number cube and then multiplying the number rolled by 2 (doubling the number). The student then records the equation on her recording sheet. After 3 rolls, each student finds the sum of her doubles products. The student with the largest sum wins the round. To challenge students to find the doubles with different factors, substitute a 5–10 number cube or spinner.

Double Up   The goal of *Double Up* (see CD) is to be the first player to find 6 different products of 2. A deck of dot cards is shuffled and placed facedown in

> **Tip**   For quick recall, remind students to think doubles when they see ×2 facts, regardless of where the 2 is located in the math fact.

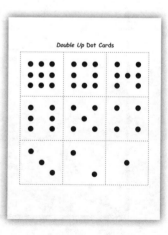

front of the players. Each player pulls a card, records the number, and doubles it on his game board. After each player pulls a card, the card is returned to the deck and shuffled again. A product can only appear once on each student's game board. A player loses his turn if he pulls a card that produces a product that he has already recorded.

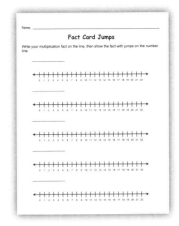

Fact Cards to Review ×2 Facts   Fact cards can be used for math fact games, center activities, or whole-class reviews. Selecting targeted math facts (e.g., ×2 fact cards) and providing short, focused reviews of those facts can be a regular addition to math time; however, rather than having students immediately shout out an answer as in traditional flash card drills, ask students to look at each fact card and think about the answer. When you raise your hand, students may call out each answer or turn and share the answer with a partner. Once students have some experience with the ×2 multiplication facts, mix in some related division facts. Following are additional fact card activities for ×2 facts.

Tip   Help students understand math fact games by playing the game with your entire class. You act as one player and the entire class is your opponent. Discuss the rules and strategies of the game and model appropriate and positive game-playing behavior.

Fact Card Jumps   Provide students with a set of fact cards for the ×2 facts and a number line recording sheet (see CD). Have students shuffle the fact cards and select a card. Students then show the fact by creating jumps on the number line (e.g., 2 × 3 is represented by 2 jumps of 3 or 4 × 2 is represented by 4 jumps of 2). Have students record the multiplication equation to go with each number line drawing (see Figure 2.5).

Student Fact Card Decks   Provide students with their own set of fact cards. Begin by giving students fact cards for ×2 facts. As new facts are introduced, give students the new facts to add to their decks. Store the decks in sealable plastic bags, using permanent marker to write students' names on the bags. The fact card bags can be used in class or taken home for additional practice. Templates for student-sized fact cards are provided on the Assessment Tools section of the CD.

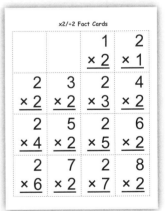

Figure 2.5 *Students randomly select a fact card and represent the fact with jumps on their number line.*

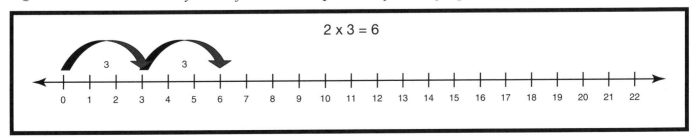

Doubles Match-Up   Have students work alone or in pairs to match addition doubles equations (4 + 4 = 8) to multiplication equations (2 × 4 = 8) and to pictures representing the doubles (see CD templates). This can be modified to include only 2 items to match (i.e., match the picture to the multiplication equation or match the addition and multiplication equations). Challenge students to match division equation cards with the corresponding picture cards (see CD).

Monitoring Progress

Monitoring students' progress toward automaticity requires ongoing and varied techniques for assessing fact mastery and tracking each student's progress. In each chapter, you will find a strategy or tip for examining students' progress and keeping them on track. Select the strategies that work for you. Tracking progress allows us to celebrate students' mastery, identify concerns, and design appropriate interventions to address those concerns.

Fact Checks   Fact Checks are brief, independent fact reviews and are one tool for monitoring automaticity with math facts. The results indicate which facts are known and unknown, and provide input into whether students are automatically recalling the fact or using other, more time-consuming, strategies to find the answers. Assessing for automaticity does mean that the time taken to complete the task is an important indicator of mastery, but keep in mind that timed tests can have a negative effect on many students. Although automaticity is a goal, we want to refrain from comparing one student's time to another's time. Rather than setting a time goal that all students' must achieve, consider using time as a personal motivator by providing a specific amount of time (e.g., two-and-a-half to three minutes) and challenging stu-

Doubles Match-Up Cards	
1 + 1 = 2	2 × 1 = 2
2 + 2 = 4	2 × 2 = 4
3 + 3 = 6	2 × 3 = 6
4 + 4 = 8	2 × 4 = 8
5 + 5 = 10	2 × 5 = 10
6 + 6 = 12	2 × 6 = 12

Doubles Match-Up Cards (cont.)	
7 + 7 = 14	2 × 7 = 14
8 + 8 = 16	2 × 8 = 16
9 + 9 = 18	2 × 9 = 18
10 + 10 = 20	2 × 10 = 20

Doubles Match-Up Cards

dents to see how many facts they can correctly answer in that amount of time, then further challenge them to "beat their own record" on the following attempt. To track their own progress, students can record the date and the number of math facts answered correctly. These data are invaluable for student-teacher conferences.

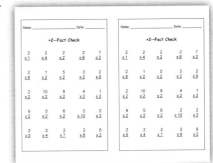

Connecting to Division

As students develop an understanding of multiplication with 2 as a factor, take every opportunity to talk about the connection between multiplication and division facts. Students might be asked to talk about the similarities and differences between the following equations:

$$2 \times 5 = 10 \qquad\qquad 10 \div 2 = 5$$

Students might focus on the similarities in the numbers in each equation (e.g., "They both have a 2, 5, and 10 in them."). They might state that they are part of a *fact family,* but pose questions that require students to delve more deeply into their thinking and explain their understanding of the equations. Colleen observed that "if you have 2 groups of 5 you get 10, but if you have 10 and split it into 2 groups, there's 5 in each group." Megan added, "2×5 is double 5, but $10 \div 2$ is splitting 10 in half."

You might provide manipulatives so students can show the operations as they discuss their ideas or have the class act out equations. Exploring the connections between the operations will help strengthen students' problem-solving skills as they deepen their understanding of the equations. Once students have a firm understanding of inverse operations and have gained fluency with their multiplication facts, they will be empowered by their expanded repertoire of division facts, too.

Students might be asked to share how they arrived at the answer to the following equation:

$$12 \div 2 = n$$

Erica shared "I just thought 2 times what number equals 12, it's 6!" When faced with a division fact that may be difficult, students can be frequently reminded to *think multiplication.*

CHAPTER THREE

Multiplying by 10

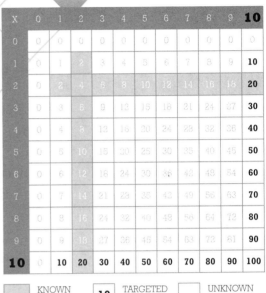

X	0	1	2	3	4	5	6	7	8	9	**10**
0	0	0	0	0	0	0	0	0	0	0	0
1	0	1	2	3	4	5	6	7	8	9	**10**
2	0	2	4	6	8	10	12	14	16	18	**20**
3	0	3	6	9	12	15	18	21	24	27	**30**
4	0	4	8	12	16	20	24	28	32	36	**40**
5	0	5	10	15	20	25	30	35	40	45	**50**
6	0	6	12	18	24	30	36	42	48	54	**60**
7	0	7	14	21	28	35	42	49	56	63	**70**
8	0	8	16	24	32	40	48	56	64	72	**80**
9	0	9	18	27	36	45	54	63	72	81	**90**
10	0	10	20	30	40	50	60	70	80	90	100

| | KNOWN FACTS | **10** TARGETED FACTS | UNKNOWN FACTS |

As we continue to explore multiplication facts, the big ideas related to numbers and operations guide our discussions. Because we are working in a base-ten number system and because of the importance of patterns within our number system, focusing on multiplication with 10 as a factor develops foundational understanding. We continue to build on the ideas already discussed and capitalize on students' strengths of counting by tens to expand their repertoire of math facts.

Focusing on the Big Ideas

In Chapter One, we identified big ideas about multiplication and division that relate to all facts. When focusing on math facts with 10 as a factor, the following big ideas have particular significance.

Multiplication by 10 is like skip-counting by 10.

Students have already discussed the connection between skip-counting and multiplication and most students have had lots of experience skip-counting by 10! Reminding students of this connection and helping them see that they already know 6 × 10 if they can skip-count (10, 20, 30, 40, 50, 60) will help them build on previous knowledge and ease anxiety for this new set of math facts. Students have most likely also had experience with base-ten blocks and ten-frames. Using these familiar tools can help students make sense of ×10 facts.

Our number system is a system of patterns.

The patterns in multiplication by 10 are quickly evident to students. When multiplying by 10, the factor and the product look similar, but the product has a 0 added to form a number with an additional place value (e.g., 5 × 10 = 50). Discussions that focus on patterns and hands-on tasks that allow students to visualize 3 tens for 3 × 10 will support their understanding of why this happens. Recognizing and making sense of patterns through observations, rather than memorizing a rule of just "adding a 0," will help students better understand these facts.

The order of the factors does not change the product (the commutative property).

Whether students are visualizing 10 groups of a certain size (e.g., 10 × 4 or 10 groups of 4), or whether they are visualizing groups of 10 items (e.g., 4 × 10 or 4 groups of 10), they will notice that the products are the same, reducing the number of math facts that need to be memorized.

These big ideas about numbers are central to students' understanding and should guide the types of questions we pose as we explore ×10 facts.

How does skip-counting by ten relate to multiplying by ten?

What patterns do you notice in the products?

When you multiply 1–10 by ten, why are the products always two-digit numbers? Why do the products have a 0 in the ones-place?

Does the order of the factors affect the product? Give examples to justify your thinking.

Our goal is to continually reinforce the big ideas related to math facts as we help students develop multiplication strategies.

Understanding ×10 Facts

Literature Link: *The Grouchy Ladybug*

The Grouchy Ladybug by Eric Carle (1977) is a children's literature classic. In this story, a grouchy ladybug spends her day picking fights with other animals before flying away. Our exploration with ×10 facts focuses on the spots on a ladybug.

Before Reading   Share the cover and title of the book with the class. Read the brief explanation of aphids and ladybugs from the front matter of the book. Ask students why they think a ladybug would be grouchy. Ask them what a ladybug might do when it is grouchy. Tell them to listen to the story to find out what this ladybug does when it is grouchy.

During Reading   As you read the story, the ladybug stops briefly to pick fights with different animals and then flies away. Ask students to predict the next animal that might appear each time the ladybug flies away.

After Reading   Provide students with some ladybug templates (see CD). Ask them to identify how many spots are on each ladybug. This is a great opportunity to inquire how they determined the number of spots. Did they count each spot? Did they count 5 on one side and double it? Could they have used their multiplication skills ($2 \times 5 = 10$) to figure out the number of spots?

Ask students to imagine that some ladybugs landed on a leaf. The students' job will be to determine the total number of spots on the leaf. Have students work with partners and pick a number from a set of 1–10 number cards (see CD template). The number students pick tells the number of ladybugs on their leaf. Have students draw a picture and write a multiplication equation for the total number of spots on their leaf (see *Ladybugs on a Leaf* activity on the CD). When they are done, have them repeat the activity two more times, picking a total of three different number cards and determining the total number of spots on the leaf for each amount of ladybugs.

After students have found the total number of spots for three different amounts of ladybugs, have them share their findings. Recording the total number of spots for 1–10 ladybugs on the board, as students share

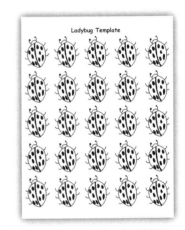

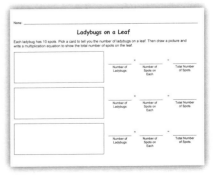

their findings, will provide students with a full set of data. Ask students to observe the data and talk with their partners about their observations (see Figure 3.1). Try prompts like:

Each ladybug has 10 spots. Tell how you can find the total number of spots if the number of ladybugs changes.

How can thinking about the spots on ladybugs help you multiply by 10?

Next, have students work with their partners to explore the following problem.

> **Ladybugs in Kim's yard have 10 spots. She catches 4 ladybugs on Tuesday, 5 ladybugs on Wednesday, and 6 ladybugs on Thursday. How many total spots did she catch each day? Explain how you know.**

Observe students as they discuss the problem with their partners. Questions like the following guide students who may be struggling with their thinking.

How many ladybugs did Kim catch each day?

How many spots did each ladybug have?

How did you figure out how many spots Kim caught on Tuesday? How do you know?

What do you notice about the connection between the number of ladybugs and the total number of spots?

Figure 3.1 *This student recognizes the connection between counting tens and multiplying by 10.*

Ladybugs on a Leaf

Each ladybug has 10 spots. Tell how you can find the total number of spots if the number of ladybugs changes.

I can just count ten each time. For example ten three times I can see that it is 30.

How can thinking about the spots on ladybugs help you multiply by 10?

It helps me because I know that there is 10 spots and if I don't Know what 10X3 is I can just count ten three times.

Ask the students to share some of the different methods they used for solving the problem. Methods might include drawing pictures, skip-counting, using repeated addition, multiplying, creating tables, or others. Take the opportunity to make connections between various methods to reinforce the big ideas of multiplication.

Exploring the Facts: Looking for Patterns

Provide each pair of students with rods (tens) from a base-ten block set. Ask partners to use the rods to find the products for ×10 facts (see the *Observing Tens* activity and base-ten templates on the CD). If students are multiplying 10 × 3, they select 3 rods, skip-count to determine the total, and then record the total, continuing the process to complete the list of ×10 facts.

Once they have completed the math facts, have students examine the facts, look for any patterns they might see, and record their observations. Once students have recorded observations, guide them in a discussion to focus on the patterns they have noticed. Students will likely notice the connection between one of the factors and the product (e.g., "You just add a 0 to the factor."). Challenge students to use their experiences with the tens rods to explain why that will always be true.

Supporting All Learners

Ladybug Hundred Charts   Provide students with some ladybug markers and a hundred chart (see CD). Each ladybug has 10 spots. Have students work with partners to show the total number of spots by placing ladybugs on a hundred chart (e.g., 1 ladybug would be placed on 10 because it has 10 spots. The next ladybug has 10 more spots, so where would it be placed?). Have students continue to place ladybugs on the space on the hundred chart that shows the total of the spots (see Figure 3.2). Have students count aloud as they tell the number of spots on 1, 2, 3, or more ladybugs. Ask students to talk with partners to discuss their observations from their hundred chart. Pose questions like the following.

What do you notice about the total number of spots and the total number of ladybugs?

What pattern do you notice about the number of spots as you add ladybugs?

Tip   Allow students to discover the rule for multiplying by 10. Hands-on experiences with base-ten blocks, coupled with observations of the factors and products, will result in students' discovering and understanding the *just add a 0* rule.

Figure 3.2 *A student places ladybugs on a hundred chart to find the product of 8 × 10.*

Hundred Chart

1	2	3	4	5	6	7	8	9	10
11	12	13	14	15	16	17	18	19	20
21	22	23	24	25	26	27	28	29	30
31	32	33	34	35	36	37	38	39	40
41	42	43	44	45	46	47	48	49	50
51	52	53	54	55	56	57	58	59	60
61	62	63	64	65	66	67	68	69	70
71	72	73	74	75	76	77	78	79	80
81	82	83	84	85	86	87	88	89	90
91	92	93	94	95	96	97	98	99	100

Relating ×10 Facts to Money   Making connections between math concepts is a valuable way to strengthen students' understanding. One dime has a value of 10 cents, so determining the value of groups of dimes is a natural connection to ×10 facts. Using In/Out charts to show the relationship between the number of dimes and the total amount of money, or cents, as in Figure 3.3, provides an effective visual of ×10 facts (see the *Dimes and Cents* activity on the CD).

Students might also work with coin manipulatives to solve problems like:

Alex had 6 dimes. How many cents did he have?

John had 8 dimes. How many cents did he have?

And don't forget to encourage students to write their own dimes and cents problems.

Posing Problems to Explore ×10 Facts   Pose problems like the following to explore ×10 facts.

> Mrs. King set up chairs for the class play. She set up 4 rows of chairs. She put 10 chairs in each row. How many chairs did Mrs. King set up for the play?

> Lisa bought 6 packages of colored pencils. There were 10 pencils in each package. How many pencils did she buy?

Figure 3.3 *Patterns become obvious as students observe the Dimes and Cents chart.*

Dimes and Cents

Complete the IN/OUT chart to show the number of dimes and the amount of money for each group of dimes. Draw a picture to show one of the rows.

Number of Dimes	Cents
1	10¢
2	20¢
3	30¢
4	40¢
5	50¢
6	60¢
7	70¢
8	80¢
9	90¢
10	100¢

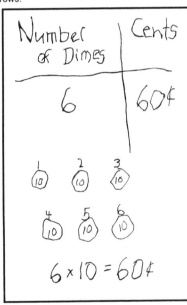

Tell about the patterns you see in the Dimes and Cents Chart above.

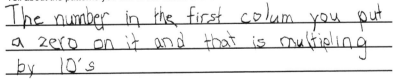

The number in the first colum you put a zero on it and that is multipling by 10's

How can you tell the total amount if you have 7 dimes?

you do 7×10=70

Encourage students to use manipulatives, draw pictures, or use other strategies to solve these problems. Talk about different ways to get the answers (e.g., skip-count, add, multiply). Record the multiplication equations on the board.

Building Automaticity

After students have engaged in a variety of activities to understand multiplying by 10, it is time to provide them with targeted practice to commit ×10 facts to memory.

Targeted Practice

Tools to Promote Accuracy   As teachers, we want our students to practice their skills in a meaningful and accurate way. After all, practicing inaccurate facts or inefficient methods does not promote fluency and leads to student frustration. Support students as they play math fact games by providing them with accuracy tools. Number lines, hundred charts, multiplication charts, or even calculators are all possible tools. The CD has many accuracy tools that can be quickly copied and distributed to students who might need the support. In many games, having opponents "check" a player's computation doubles the practice. Games can be modified so that inaccurate calculations result in losing a turn or removing a game piece from the board. Providing accuracy tools places the emphasis on mastery of the facts.

Top Tens   Provide each pair of students with a 1–6 number cube and a *Top Tens* recording sheet (see CD). Students take turns rolling the number cube and then multiplying the number rolled by 10. The student then records the equation on his sheet. After 3 rolls, each student finds his sum. The student with the largest sum wins the round. To vary the game, substitute a 5–10 number cube or use a 1–10 spinner to practice with different factors.

Keep It, Toss It   In *Keep It, Toss It* (see game template on CD), students spin a spinner and multiply the result by 10. They then decide if they want to keep their product or toss it. Products are recorded in the appropriate column of their score sheet. Players may only spin a total of 10 spins. After 5 products are recorded in the Keep It column, the products are added to find the player's total score. The player with the highest score wins. Students can use calculators to help them find the sum of their Keep It column.

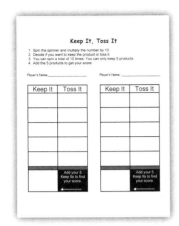

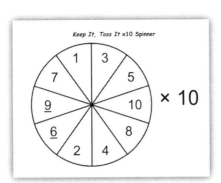

Partner Fact Card Practice Encourage students to practice facts with partners. This allows you to work with a small group of students who may be experiencing more difficulty with the facts or to conference with individual students to assess their knowledge. Remember to add some fact cards from previously taught math facts (e.g., ×2 facts) to ensure continued review.

Creating ×10 Fact Grids Provide each student with centimeter grid paper (see CD). As students pick a fact card, have them create an area model for the fact by outlining a section on the grid paper (i.e., 4 × 10 would be represented by outlining a section that is 4 across and 10 down or vice versa). Have students record the equation in each outlined area. Students can continue to do this until their grid is filled, and then have them grab a new grid and keep going! You might vary this activity by having students cut out the areas and glue them to construction paper to create ×10 posters.

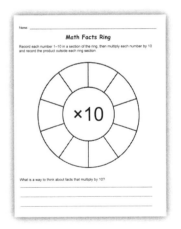

Math Facts Rings *Math Facts Rings* (see CD) are another quick practice activity. Have students record the numbers 1–10 in random order in the sections of each ring. Students then multiply each number by 10 and record the products outside each ring section.

Monitoring Progress: More on Fact Checks

Fact Checks are one way to check for mastery, particularly when assessing automaticity, but should not be overused or overemphasized. A variety of Fact Checks are provided on the CD to allow you to select those that fit your goals. Some of the Fact Checks target specific fact sets (e.g., ×10 facts). You will also find Fact Checks that target related multiplication and division facts to allow students to practice these facts together. These multi-operation fact checks contain 50 facts and require students to shift from one operation to

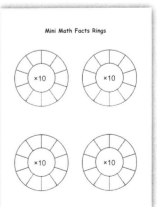

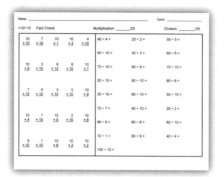

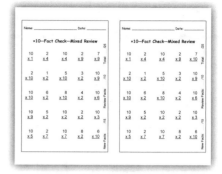

another, so students should be given additional time to complete them (e.g., $5\frac{1}{2}$–6 minutes). Mixed Fact Checks, which assess both current and previously learned facts, are organized to allow teachers to easily score the current facts and previously learned facts separately. The columns on the ends and the center column measure the current facts, and the other two columns measure previously learned facts. Simply tallying correct responses in each column will give a quick view of progress.

Tip **Tip for Tracking Progress**

Provide students with a blank multiplication chart (see CD). After numerous activities to develop facts, have students record their known facts on their charts. Collect their charts or have students keep charts in a safe place (i.e., glued inside the cover of a math journal) so students can add to the charts as they master more facts.

Connecting to Division

Division with Ladybugs

The Grouchy Ladybug activity from earlier in this chapter can be modified for division facts. Students explore problems such as:

> There are 80 dots altogether. If there are 10 dots on each ladybug, how many ladybugs are there?

Pose different dot totals and have students determine the number of ladybugs. After exploration, students can examine the pattern of the quotients when working with divisors of 10.

Exploring Division with Manipulatives

Base-ten blocks can be used to provide a hands-on exploration of division. Provide each group of students with 4 rods (tens) from a base-ten block set. After counting how many units (ones) there are altogether (40), ask students how many units would be in each group if they divided the 40 into 4 equal groups. Students should be encouraged to record an equation that shows what they did. Ideas can be shared and recorded on the board. This exploration can be repeated a few times, changing the total and the number of groups. After the final exploration, encourage talk and writing to summarize students' insights.

How are these equations like equations that multiply by 10?

How are they different from equations that multiply by 10?

How could knowing how to multiply by 10 help us solve these problems?

Tip It is important for students to understand the concepts of multiplication and division; however, when the focus is on math fact fluency, remind students to *think multiplication*. Mastering multiplication facts and exploring fact families support students' mastery of division facts.

Write to Divide

In *Write to Divide*, students create their own game. Students write numbers 1–10 in twelve boxes, keeping in mind that not every number needs to be used and a number can be used more than one time (see *Write to Divide* activity on CD). After players fill their boxes, they take turns spinning numbers and dividing by 10. If the quotient is in one of their boxes, they cross it out. Only one number can be crossed out per spin. Players take turns spinning and the first player to cross out all of their numbers wins the game.

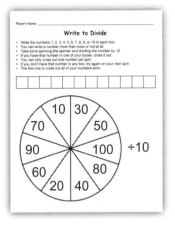

CHAPTER FOUR

Multiplying by 5

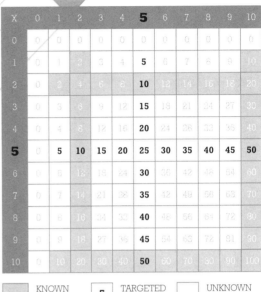

X	0	1	2	3	4	**5**	6	7	8	9	10
0	0	0	0	0	0	0	0	0	0	0	0
1	0	1	2	3	4	5	6	7	8	9	10
2	0	2	4	6	8	10	12	14	16	18	20
3	0	3	6	9	12	15	18	21	24	27	30
4	0	4	8	12	16	20	24	28	33	36	40
5	0	5	10	15	20	25	30	35	40	45	50
6	0	6	12	18	24	30	36	42	48	54	60
7	0	7	14	21	28	35	42	49	56	63	70
8	0	8	16	24	32	40	48	56	64	72	80
9	0	9	18	27	36	45	54	63	72	81	90
10	0	10	20	30	40	50	60	70	80	90	100

KNOWN FACTS   **5** TARGETED FACTS   UNKNOWN FACTS

Math facts with 5 as a factor build on students' previously learned math facts skills. Just as with the ×2 and ×10 facts, patterns are a powerful way to learn ×5 facts. Students' extensive experience skip-counting by fives provides them with essential prior knowledge to master these facts. In addition, real-world connections, like five fingers on a hand or five pennies in a nickel, are commonplace, so our students have experience thinking in fives. And now that students have explored the ×10 facts, they can use this knowledge to better understand ×5 facts, thinking of them as half of the related ×10 fact.

Focusing on the Big Ideas

When focusing on multiplication with 5 as a factor, some big ideas that support students in developing critical strategies include the following.

Multiplication by 5 is like skip-counting by 5.

Students have already explored the connection between skip-counting and multiplication, and most students have had lots of experience skip-counting by fives. Reminding students of this connection, and helping them recognize that they already know the product of 5 × 6 if they can skip-count 5, 10, 15, 20, 25, 30, will help them build on their previous knowledge and ease their anxiety about learning this new set of math facts.

Our number system is a system of patterns.

Patterns in multiplication by 5 are immediately evident to students. Students quickly notice that all of the products have either a 0 or 5 in the ones place and that the products alternate between even numbers and odd numbers. Observing, discussing, and generalizing about patterns helps students make sense of the ×5 facts.

5 is half of 10. Multiplying a number by 5 will result in a product that is half of the product that results when the same number is multiplied by 10.

From their earlier experiences with counting, addition, and subtraction, students have developed an understanding of 10 and have internalized the concept that 5 is half of 10. We have 10 fingers, 5 on each hand. A ten-frame is made up of 2 five-frames. In a hundred chart, each row consists of 10 numbers, 2 sets of 5. This understanding helps students figure out ×5 facts from known ×10 facts by simply cutting the product in half.

The order of the factors does not change the product (the commutative property).

Whether students are visualizing 5 groups of a certain size (e.g., 5 × 4 or 5 groups of 4) or whether they are visualizing groups of 5 (e.g., 4 × 5 or 4 groups of 5), they notice that the products are the same. Continued investigations with the commutative property build students' confidence that the order of the factors does not change the product.

These big ideas about numbers are central to students' understanding and should guide the types of questions we pose to stimulate discussions about ×5 facts.

What patterns do you notice in the products when you multiply by 5?

How do the products for ×5 facts connect to the products for ×10 facts?

If you forget a ×5 fact, could you find the answer by knowing the related ×10 fact? How?

Does the order of the factors affect the product? Give examples to justify your thinking.

Understanding ×5 Facts

Exploring the Facts: An Investigation with Pennies

To begin an exploration of ×5 facts, students work with partners to determine the amount of money in sets of piggy banks. Provide partners with the piggy bank work mat (see CD) and at least 50 pennies, then pose the following problem.

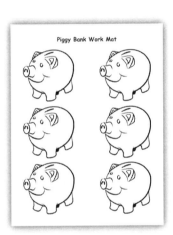

Piggy Bank Work Mat

> Mrs. Alexander bought each of her 7 grandchildren a brand new piggy bank. She went to the bank to get enough pennies to put 5 pennies in each of their piggy banks. How many pennies did she need?

Have students work together to solve the problem using their pennies, then have students share their solutions with the class. Probe with questions like the following.

How many piggy banks did she have?

How did you find the total number of pennies she needed?

After you placed the pennies in each bank, did you count all of the pennies to find the total? Were there other ways you might have found the total?

Did anyone skip-count to find the total? Which way would be faster, skip-counting or counting all of the pennies? Why?

Did anyone add to find the total number of pennies? Why would addition work to solve this problem?

Did anyone multiply? What multiplication math fact would help you solve this problem?

Record on the board *7 × 5 = 35* as you verbalize "7 groups of 5 pennies is 35 pennies" or "7 piggy banks with 5 pennies in each bank is 35 total pennies."

Challenge students to work with partners to find the total number of pennies needed for 1–10 piggy banks and to write multiplication equations to show their answers (e.g., $1 \times 5 = 5$, $2 \times 5 = 10$, etc.). Remind students that Mrs. Alexander wants each bank to hold exactly 5 pennies. Tell students that they may use the pennies and banks if it helps them find the totals, or they may find the totals in another way, but their goal is to find the products for the ×5 facts.

Once students have completed their charts, have them share the ×5 facts as you record them on the board. Then, ask students to work with partners to observe for patterns. Have them share their insights with the class. Their insights are likely to include:

- The ones digit is always 0 or 5.
- The products alternate odd, then even.
- Some of the products are ×10 products.
- Every other product is a ×10 product.

Challenge students to talk about why these patterns appear.

Does it make sense that every other ×5 product is a ×10 product? Why? Why would every other product be even? Could it be related to what happens when you add 5+5?

End the lesson by asking each student to write one insight about ×5 facts as in Figure 4.1.

What have they learned?
What will help them master these facts?

Tip Connections to real-world experiences provide insights about ×5 facts. Finding the value of sets of nickels or determining the minutes that have passed when the minute hand is on the 4 shows students everyday examples of multiplication by 5.

Figure 4.1 *This student shares insights for finding ×5 products.*

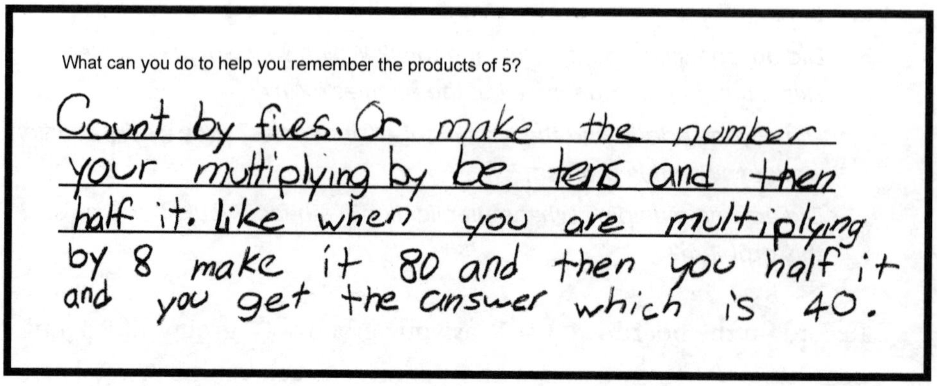

What can you do to help you remember the products of 5?

Count by fives. Or make the number your multiplying by be tens and then half it. like when you are multiplying by 8 make it 80 and then you half it and you get the answer which is 40.

Literature Link: *Count on Pablo*

In *Count on Pablo*, by Barbara deRubertis (1999), Pablo and his grandmother prepare and sell vegetables at an outdoor market. The story provides a review of previously taught math facts as well as an exploration of ×5 facts as Pablo and his grandmother sell onions tied in pairs (×2 facts), tomatoes in boxes of 10 (×10 facts), and peppers in bags of 5 (×5 facts). Pablo skip-counts to determine the number of vegetables being prepared for market, but through classroom explorations, the story allows for an easy transition from skip-counting to multiplication.

Before Reading Do a picture walk through the book, showing students the illustrations and asking them to predict what the story might be about. Discuss outdoor markets at which vendors sell their fresh fruits and vegetables.

Ask students to think about their experiences at grocery stores. Are fruits and vegetables sold individually or are they sometimes sold in packages? Why might they be sold in groups or packages?

During Reading As you read the story, be sure to emphasize the way in which the vegetables are packed for sale at the market (e.g., individually, pairs, groups of 5 or 10). Encourage students to join in as Pablo skip-counts throughout the story.

After Reading Ask students a few comprehension questions to be sure they understand some of the key aspects of the story.

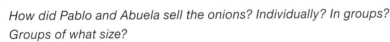

> *How did Pablo and Abuela sell the onions? Individually? In groups?*
> *Groups of what size?*
> *How did Pablo and Abuela package the tomatoes?*
> *How did Pablo and Abuela package the peppers?*

Provide students with a fifty chart (see CD) and some transparent counters. Have them choose a color counter (e.g., red) to show ×10 facts by placing counters on the correct products as you review 1 × 10, 2 × 10, 3 × 10, 4 × 10, and 5 × 10. Ask students to think about the counters as Pablo's boxes of tomatoes. The first counter covers the number of tomatoes in 1 box, the second covers the number of tomatoes in 2 boxes, and so on. Have students refer to the fifty chart to tell you the number of tomatoes in 1, 2, 3, 4, and 5 boxes. This would be a great opportunity to introduce, or reinforce, the meaning of the word *multiples*. Explain that products are also called *multiples*. Their red counters are covering *multiples of 10*,

Fifty Chart

1	2	3	4	5	6	7	8	9	10
11	12	13	14	15	16	17	18	19	20
21	22	23	24	25	26	27	28	29	30
31	32	33	34	35	36	37	38	39	40
41	42	43	44	45	46	47	48	49	50

Tip A classroom word wall is a great way to display new math vocabulary as it appears in your lessons.

or any number that is a product when you multiply by 10. For example 10, 20, 30, 40 are all multiples of 10 because they are products of a number multiplied by 10.

Have students remove the counters from their fifty chart. Tell students they will be using a different-color transparent counter (e.g., green) to show the number of peppers in Pablo's bags. Guide students' thinking with the following questions.

> *Will they be placing counters on every tenth number? Why or why not?*
> *Where will they place counters?*
> *How many peppers are in each bag?*

Have students show Pablo's counting of the peppers by placing green counters on the fifty chart (e.g., placing counters on 5, 10, 15, 20, etc.). Have students turn and share their observations of their charts with a partner. What do they notice? This time, counters are placed on every fifth number or each counter represents 5 numbers. Begin a chart of ×5 facts on the board, asking students to help you complete it by finding the products on their fifty chart. As you record each ×5 fact, ask students to tell you the product. Clarify each fact with words and symbols saying "So, one group of 5 is . . . ?" as you record *1 × 5 = 5*. Continue to record and state each fact until the chart has facts from 1–10.

When the ×5 fact list is completed, ask students to keep the green counters on the multiples of 5 on their fifty charts, but replace the red counters on the multiples of 10. Inform them that there may be more than 1 counter on a number. Ask them to turn to their partners and share their observations about the charts. Have a class discussion of their observations, being sure to ask them to explain why some numbers are both multiples of 5 and 10.

Extend the lesson by posing the following problem for students to discuss with their partners. Remind students that you will be asking them to share their solutions as well as how they arrived at their solutions.

> **If Pablo sold 8 pairs of onions, how many onions did he sell?**

Move through the room to listen to partners' discussions. Ask students to share their solutions and record some of their methods on the board (e.g., drawing pictures, skip-counting, adding, multiplying). Acknowledge that all of the methods work, but talk about how quickly students who knew the multiplication fact (8 × 2) were able to find the solution. Then, pose the following problem.

Tip **Manipulative Tip**
If transparent counters are not available, students might place small paper clips or beans on each number. Selecting transparent or small manipulatives allows students to still view the numbers on the chart.

> **If Pablo sold 5 boxes of tomatoes, how many tomatoes did he sell?**

Before students begin the task, as them to silently show you, by holding up the correct number of fingers, how many tomatoes are in each box. Quickly scan the room to be sure students understand that each box holds 10 tomatoes. Then, move through the room to listen to partners' discussions as they solve the problem. Have them share their solutions with the class and again, record their methods and reinforce the efficiency of using multiplication (5×10) to find the solution. Finally, pose the following problem.

> **If Pablo sold 4 bags of peppers, how many peppers did he sell?**

Again check for understanding of peppers being in bags of 5, by asking students to show the number of peppers in a bag by holding up the appropriate number of fingers. Then, challenge students to decide on the multiplication fact that would solve the problem (see Figure 4.2).

Pose a final problem for students to turn and share with a partner.

Figure 4.2 *Student A uses pictures to make sense of the problem, and student B uses an understanding of the connection to skip-counting.*

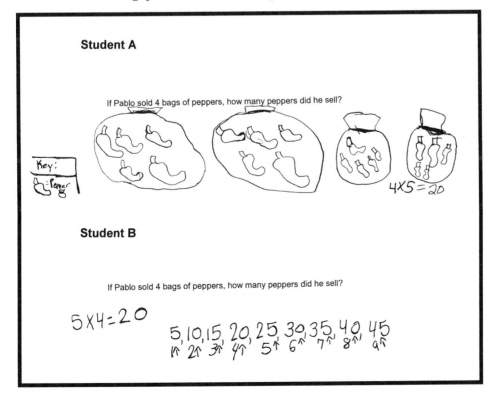

> Pablo had 23 peppers and decided to sell them in groups of 5. Could he sell all of his peppers that way? Why?

Move through the room to listen to students' mathematical talk. Are they using their fifty chart to see if 23 is covered? Are they skip-counting by fives to see if 23 is named? Are they referring to the list of ×5 facts to see if 23 appears? Are they grouping the counters to test their thinking? Are they noticing that 23 does not end in a 0 or 5? Have students share their thoughts in a class discussion. Then, ask students to write in their journals with this prompt.

> Danny says 23 is a multiple of 5. Do you agree or disagree? Explain your thinking.

Supporting All Learners

Team Problems   Many students respond to team problem-solving tasks in which they can hear others' thinking and test their ideas. A problem card related to the ×5 facts (see CD) is given to each team of three or four students. Students work together to solve the problem. Team members must write a multiplication equation to solve their problem and must also show the solution in at least one other way (e.g., using manipulatives, drawing pictures, skip-counting, etc.). Team members raise their hands when a problem is solved, the teacher checks the solution and their thinking, and then hands the students another problem card. Groups move through the problems at their own pace. After a set amount of time, solutions and strategies can be shared with the class, but whole-class sharing is not necessary if the teacher has met with individual teams to hear students' thinking as they solve each problem. Varying the complexity of the problems will give you the flexibility to assign problems that best match the needs of each team. Problems may include:

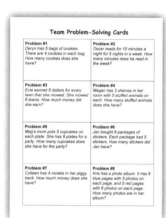

> Deryn has 5 bags of cookies. There are 4 cookies in each bag. How many cookies does she have?

> Oscar reads for 10 minutes each night for 5 nights. How many minutes does he read altogether?

> Kris has a photo album. It has 8 blue pages with 5 photos on each page, and 5 red pages with 6 photos on each page. How many photos are in her album?

Chanting Facts   Rhythmically chanting math facts, or setting math facts to familiar songs, may be helpful for some students, particularly those with attention problems or other learning difficulties. Chanting math facts in a rhythmic way requires students to repeatedly verbalize a set of facts (i.e., 1 times 5 is 5, 2 times 5 is 10, 3 times 5 is 15, etc.). Some students respond well to singing the facts to familiar tunes like "The Farmer in the Dell." Just be sure that students are focusing on the ideas and not simply chanting or singing words. Fluency is only one part of math fact mastery. Without a foundation of understanding, memory can be very fleeting.

Making Connection to Money Concepts   Ideas for relating ×10 facts to money were shared in Chapter Three and can be easily adapted for ×5 facts. For ×5 facts, students connect the number of nickels to the total amount of money, so 4 nickels would total 4 × 5 or 20 cents, because each nickel represents 5 cents. The *Dimes and Cents* activity for ×10 facts has been modified to a *Nickels and Cents* activity (see CD) to strengthen ×5 facts. Allowing students to use nickel manipulatives will support students who still need to explore the facts in a hands-on way.

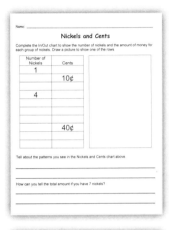

The *How Much Money?* activity (see the CD) challenges students to compare the values of similar quantities of nickels and dimes. This activity continues to build students' number sense as it supports the development of the big idea that multiples of 5 are half of multiples of 10.

Making Connections to Concepts About Time   Facts that have 5 as a factor provide an excellent opportunity to connect the concepts of multiplication and telling time. The numbers on a clock symbolize 5-minute increments (e.g., the 4 on a clock face represents 20 minutes because there are 4 groups of 5 minutes). Students can use movable clocks to represent different math facts. Students might begin by moving the minute hand of the clock to each number on the clock face while skip-counting by fives, then progress to writing multiplication equations that connect the number on the clock face to the number of minutes.

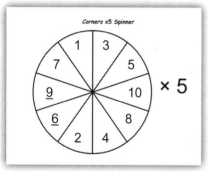

Building Automaticity

Targeted Practice

Introducing Math Games   To maximize the impact of math fact games, model the games with the class before students have the opportunity to play games with partners. Games can be modeled on an overhead, on a SMART Board, or with a document camera to allow students to both see and hear the rules. During modeling, explain the rules and explore possible strategies, or thinking points, for the game. Field questions about the rules of the game or what to do when different scenarios arise. Have students play the game with partners as you move through the room observing students' understanding of the rules. A thorough introduction to each game will result in smoother play when students are working on their own.

Corners   *Corners* (see CD) provides students with targeted practice for ×5 facts. Players take turns spinning a spinner and multiplying the number by 5. Students then place a counter, or bean, on a space on the board with that product. The goal of this game is to cover 4 adjacent spaces to form the 4 corners of a square.

Ratio Tables   Provide students with a vertical In/Out (ratio) table and ask them to record the product for each fact as in the *Math Facts Column* activity on the CD. These tables spur discussions and prompt writing about patterns seen in the rows or columns. Ratio tables can also be used to explore real-world connections (e.g., 5 points on a star or 5 toes on a foot (see CD activity)). And feel free to vary the format to create rows instead of columns. Whether tables are vertical or horizontal, they provide nice repetition of the facts.

Tip   Using beans or counters to cover game boards, rather than marking off products with pens or markers, allows students to clear the board and begin again each time they complete a game. Games that allow for repeated play are providing repeated practice with math facts!

Tip   Once students have experience completing In/Out tables in which the In column is organized (numbers progressing from 1–10), mix the order of the numbers in the In column, so students cannot rely on patterns to complete the table and must rely on their math fact knowledge.

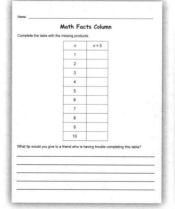

Fact Card Arrays   Provide students with a set of ×5 fact cards and a set of 50 counters. Have students select a fact card and make an array to represent the fact. Students count the number of rows, the number of counters in each row, and the total number of counters, and then record their data. Remind students that skip-counting, or simply knowing the multiplication fact, are more efficient ways to find the total rather than counting every individual counter.

Independent Fact Card Reviews   The following activities minimize the stress sometimes associated with fact card practice, as they emphasize knowledge of the answer rather than speed. Suggest one of the following for students who need additional practice with the ×5 facts.

Pick a card, or a designated number of cards, and . . .

- Draw an array of the fact.

- Write the repeated addition sentence that goes with it.

- Write the fact, with the product, three times.

- Write a story problem for the fact.

Monitoring Progress: Working Toward Automaticity

Giving students frequent opportunities to engage in independent fact reviews provides them with repeated practice, supports fluency, and allows for ongoing monitoring of each student's progress toward automaticity. Fact Checks might focus specifically on the fact being taught (e.g., ×5 facts) or might combine previously learned facts (e.g., ×2, ×10, and ×5 facts). The same Fact Check can be done numerous times as students work toward fluency.

Our goal for students is automaticity with math facts, but automaticity takes time. Students benefit from frequent practice and lots of teacher support (see Figure 4.3). Students can be more successful if they learn their math facts in manageable pieces and progress at reasonable rates. In this book, fact groups are sequenced so that students have a manageable number of facts to focus on at any given time, and those facts have natural connections to students' previous learning. A large menu of possible activities allows you to continue work on a fact set if students are having difficulty mastering it. Don't rush! Long-term retention is the goal.

Tip   Practice activities from previous chapters can be easily adapted for ×5 facts. You might want to try:

Fact Card Jumps (Chapter Two)

Fact Grids (Chapter Three)

Tip   Following Fact Checks, have students use yellow highlighters to indicate known facts on a completed multiplication chart (see CD). By highlighting known facts, students will also be able to quickly focus on facts that still need to be mastered. Encourage students to select a few facts as their goal for the next Fact Check.

Figure 4.3 *This teacher frequently monitors student progress and provides ongoing support.*

Connecting to Division

Linking to *Count on Pablo*

The activities for *Count on Pablo* (deRubertis 1999) can be easily modified to focus on division facts. Pablo and his grandmother put 5 peppers in each bag to take to the market. Possible division problems include:

> Pablo has 30 peppers. How many bags does he need?

> Pablo has 45 peppers in bags. How many bags of peppers does Pablo have?

These problems are wonderful opportunities for students to work with partners, use manipulatives, draw pictures, and write equations to solve division problems. They also provide a wonderful opportunity for students to connect their ideas about division with their understanding of multiplication.

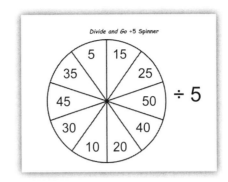

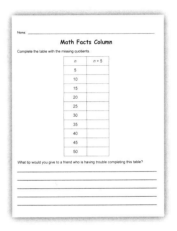

Divide and Go

Students can practice their division facts by playing *Divide and Go* (see CD). Players spin a spinner and divide by 5. The quotient is the amount of points they earn for that turn. Players accumulate and keep track of their points using a counter on a hundred chart. For example, a player has her counter on 24. She spins 45 and divides by 5 to get 9 points. She then moves her counter to 33. The first player to get to exactly 100, without going over, is the winner.

Modifying Multiplication Activities

An In/Out table can be used to help students build automaticity with multiplication facts. By changing the function on the table, it becomes an opportunity for practicing division facts (see the *Math Facts Column* activity on the CD).

Multiplying by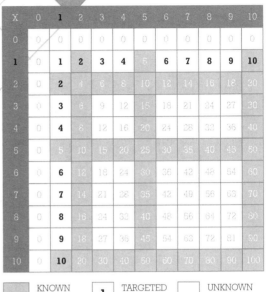

O ur students' experiences with 2, 5, and 10 as factors provide a foundation for understanding math facts and developing appropriate math facts strategies. Once students have explored math facts with these familiar groupings, we extend their understanding by introducing multiplication with 1 as a factor. Mastery of these facts is quite easy for students, although the concept of 1 as a group, or groups of 1, is a bit tough to visualize. Beginning with explorations of 2, 5, and 10 allow students to absorb the grouping concept in a more understandable context and paves the way for the unconventional idea of groups of 1.

X	0	1	2	3	4	5	6	7	8	9	10
0	0	0	0	0	0	0	0	0	0	0	0
1	0	1	2	3	4	5	6	7	8	9	10
2	0	2	4	6	8	10	12	14	16	18	20
3	0	3	6	9	12	15	18	21	24	27	30
4	0	4	8	12	16	20	24	28	32	36	40
5	0	5	10	15	20	25	30	35	40	45	50
6	0	6	12	18	24	30	36	42	48	54	60
7	0	7	14	21	28	35	42	49	56	63	70
8	0	8	16	24	32	40	48	56	64	72	80
9	0	9	18	27	36	45	54	63	72	81	90
10	0	10	20	30	40	50	60	70	80	90	100

KNOWN FACTS   1 TARGETED FACTS   UNKNOWN FACTS

Focusing on the Big Ideas

When focusing on multiplication with 1 as a factor, the following are some big ideas.

When multiplying by 1, the product is the same as the other factor.

This is known as the identity property of multiplication. Our goal is to help all students understand the reasoning behind this property. After working with basic facts, instruction can be extended so that students understand that this concept applies to any number (e.g., $241 \times 1 = 241$).

The order of the factors does not change the product (the commutative property).

Whether students are visualizing 1 group of a certain size (e.g., 1×5 or 1 group of 5) or whether they are visualizing groups of 1 (e.g., 5×1 or 5 groups of 1), they notice that the products are the same.

These big ideas about numbers are central to students' understanding and should guide the types of questions we pose during class or small-group discussions.

> *What does it mean to multiply by 1?*
>
> *What does it mean to have 1 set? Why would the product be the same as the number of items in that set?*
>
> *What patterns do you notice in the products?*
>
> *Does the order of the factors affect the product? Give examples to justify your thinking.*
>
> *Explain the connection between this multiplication equation and the related division equation.*

Our goal is to continually reinforce the big ideas related to math facts as we help students develop multiplication strategies.

Tip Strategic questioning challenges students to think about numbers, properties, and patterns as they develop math fact understanding.

Understanding ×1 Facts

Literature Link: *One Tiny Turtle*

Exploring ×1 facts through a story-related investigation provides students with an immediate context for multiplication with 1 as a factor. *One Tiny Turtle* by Nicole Davies (2001) provides a perfect context for exploring single sets as students consider the number of turtle eggs in 1 nest.

Before Reading   Prior to reading the story, talk with students about sea turtles. Ask what they know (K) about sea turtles. Ask what they want to know (W) about turtles. Have students record some K and W responses on a KWL chart (see template on CD).

During Reading   When reading the story to students for the first time, move through the story without too many interruptions for discussion. A rereading of the story will allow you to pose related math problems.

After Reading   Provide each pair or small group of students with a bag of counters and a small paper plate to represent a turtle nest. Ask students to select some counters (eggs) and place them in the nest. The students then work together to count the number of eggs in the nest, draw a picture of the nest and eggs on their recording sheet (see *Tiny Turtle Eggs* on CD), and write the multiplication equation to go with their picture (e.g., *1 × 3 = 3* if 3 eggs are in their nest). Then, the students remove the eggs and try a different number of eggs in their nest, repeating the process of counting, drawing, and recording what they see.

After groups of students have found the number of eggs in several nests, the group members share their findings. Record the multiplication equations on the board so all students can view them. Ask students to observe the factors and products in the multiplication equations.

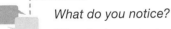

> *What do you notice?*
>
> *What is the same in each equation? What is different?*

Pose some scenarios with larger numbers of eggs in a turtle nest. Challenge students' thinking with questions like the following.

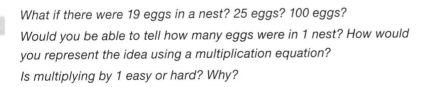

> *What if there were 19 eggs in a nest? 25 eggs? 100 eggs?*
>
> *Would you be able to tell how many eggs were in 1 nest? How would you represent the idea using a multiplication equation?*
>
> *Is multiplying by 1 easy or hard? Why?*

Ask students to work with a partner to complete their KWL charts by writing a few things they learned about turtles and about multiplication with 1 as a factor (see Figure 5.1). Have students share their ideas with the class.

Figure 5.1 *This student explains why multiplying by 1 is easy.*

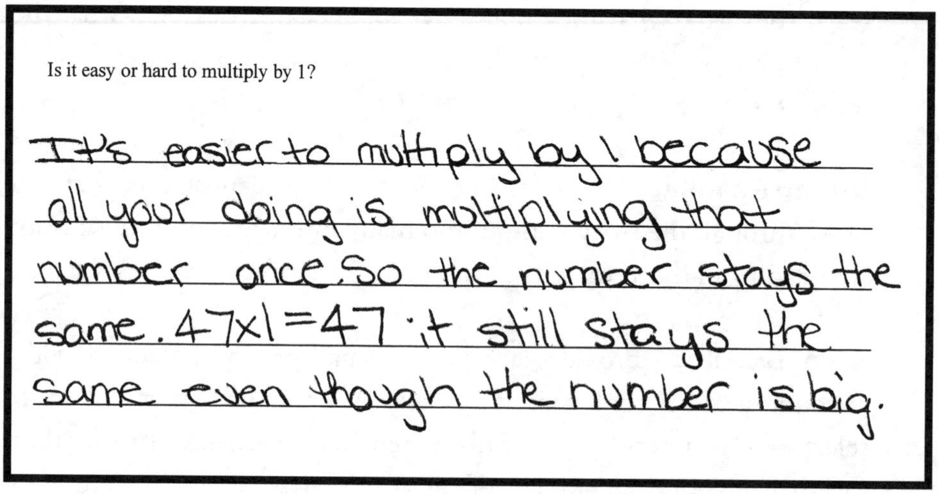

Is it easy or hard to multiply by 1?

It's easier to multiply by 1 because all your doing is multiplying that number once. So the number stays the same. 47x1=47 it still stays the same even though the number is big.

Exploring the Facts: Using Color Tiles

Create 10 bags of color tiles or cubes by placing 1 green, 2 red, and 5 yellow tiles in each transparent plastic sandwich bag. Note that the number of tiles in the bags provides a review of ×2 and ×5 facts. Pose questions to students about the total number of tiles in bags like the following.

> How many yellow tiles are in 3 bags? (3 × 5 = 15)

> How many red tiles are in 6 bags? (6 × 2 = 12)

Allow students to count the tiles to find the products, if necessary. Using a think-aloud technique, build equations to represent each situation (i.e., "So there are 3 bags with 5 yellow tiles in each bag, so I think I will write *3 × 5* for 3 groups of 5.") Record the equations.

Pose some problems about the number of green tiles in the bags. Record the equations (i.e., "How many green tiles are in 4 bags?" *4 × 1 = 4*). Ask students if there is an easier way than counting to find the total number of green tiles in a set of bags. Ask students if they can decide on a rule for ×1 facts (see Figure 5.2).

Supporting All Learners

Exploring Misunderstandings Students have already developed an understanding of adding 1 and know that the sum is simply the next counting number. Students can be so comfortable with that concept, that they inadver-

Figure 5.2 *This student explains her simple rule for multiplying by 1.*

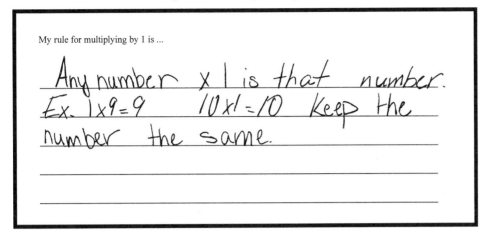

My rule for multiplying by 1 is ...

Any number x 1 is that number.
Ex. 1x9=9   10x1=10   Keep the
number the same.

tently add 1 when faced with multiplication by 1. Highlight the similarities and differences in equations by engaging students in discussions:

$$3 \times 1 = 3 \qquad\qquad\qquad 3 + 1 = 4$$

Students will certainly notice that the numbers in each equation are alike, but the symbols are different. Be sure students understand how the symbols change the meanings of each equation. Provide students with manipulatives to represent each equation or select a few students and act out the equations. Ultimately, remind students to be observant of the symbols that indicate the operation.

Another approach to addressing this misunderstanding is to ask students to write story problems about the different operations (See *What's the Problem?* on the CD). Have students label their stories with the correct equation (e.g., $1 \times 6 = n$ or $1 + 6 = n$). For 1×6, students might write "Jacqui had 1 bag of candy. There were 6 pieces in her bag. How many pieces of candy did she have?" but for $1 + 6$, students might write "John had 1 piece of candy and Jan had 6 pieces of candy. How much did they have together?"

The student in Figure 5.3 shows a misunderstanding of 3×1. In her story, Janai ate 3 bowls of ice cream and then her friend Keyonna wanted 1. Janai wants to know how many they had, but addition, not multiplication, would answer her question. Although the $\times 1$ facts are easy to memorize, students often confuse adding 1 and multiplying by 1. For students who struggle with the concepts, writing stories as a small group, with teacher guidance and a think-aloud approach, is helpful.

Figure 5.3 *This student drew a picture to represent the product she saw in the equation (3), but her story reveals a misunderstanding of 3 × 1.*

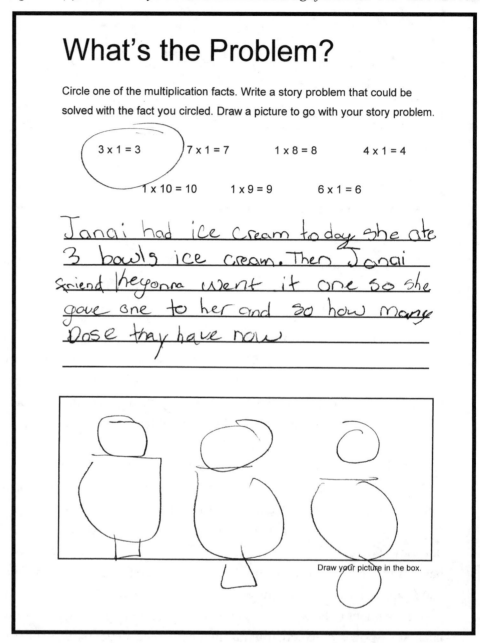

Acting Out ×1 Facts   In the literature exploration with *One Tiny Turtle*, students built equations based on 1 set of turtle eggs. All of the equations followed the pattern 1 × _ = _. Remind students that they found the total for 1 nest of 5 eggs and 1 nest of 7 eggs and 1 nest of 9 eggs, and so on. Have students share what they discovered about the product when there is just 1 group.

But what if there are many groups, with just 1 in each group? Remind students that multiplication is about *like* groups. They have explored groups of 2, 5, and 10 objects. Can there be a group of 1 object? Allow students to discuss this, acknowledging that it does not seem to make a lot of sense to think about a group of 1, but in multiplication, that is what we mean when we say 5 × 1.

Explore the idea by acting out some scenarios and recording the ×1 equations. Gather some everyday objects (e.g., crayons, pencils, erasers, lollipops). Tell students that you will be working together to find the products of ×1 facts. Give 1 pencil to each of 3 students. Record *3 × 1 = 3*. Give 1 pencil to each of 7 students and record *7 × 1 = 7*. Continue until students can easily tell you each product and can generalize for 17 or 22 students. Have them tell you a rule for ×1.

Building Automaticity

After students have engaged in a variety of activities to understand multiplication with 1 as a factor, it is time to provide students with repeated opportunities to practice the facts. Remind students that the product is the same as the other factor whenever 1 is a factor in a multiplication equation, regardless of the order of the factors. This understanding makes automaticity with ×1 facts a simple task.

Targeted Practice

Targeting Facts   After introducing a new set of facts (e.g., ×1 facts), select just those fact cards for the first rounds of practice. After several days of targeted practice with the new facts, incorporate previously learned facts to provide a balanced review.

The Teacher's Role During Game Time   While students play games, you might be observing their play or capitalizing on the opportunity to work with specific students. Watching students as they play games (see Figure 5.4) will allow you to gain insights about their fluency with math facts. Walking through the room and watching students' interactions will allow you to see who has mastered facts and who needs additional support.

Although those observations are extremely helpful, it might also be beneficial to seize the opportunity to address the needs of specific students. As most students are developing their rapid recall of facts through the games, you might be conducting small-group assessments, leading intervention groups, or conducting individual interviews (see CD). Think about both assessment and instruction as you balance opportunities to observe, assess, and reteach.

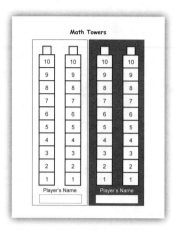

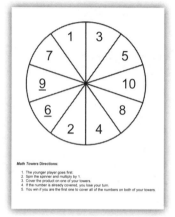

Figure 5.4 *The teacher observes students as they play a game, listening for accuracy and evidence of strategic thinking.*

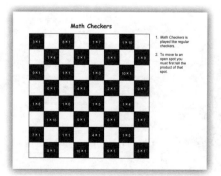

Tip **Focused Practice**

Practice with problematic facts allows for more repetition of those facts. Students can be given the job of finding their focus facts in their deck of fact cards by selecting those facts that were missed on their most recent Fact Check.

Math Towers In *Math Towers* (see template on CD), students take turns spinning a number and multiplying by 1. Students then place a marker on that floor of one of their towers. If the number is already covered on both towers, the player loses his turn. The first player to cover all of the levels of both of his towers is the winner.

Math Checkers *Math Checkers* is played like regular checkers, but in order to move to a vacant spot, a player must read the multiplication fact and name the correct product. The CD contains an example of *Math Checkers* that focuses on ×1 facts. This game offers an excellent opportunity for fact review by creating game boards that mix new facts with previously learned ones. Simply use the customizable feature on the CD to click on any space and edit the fact before printing the game board.

Monitoring Progress: Teacher-Administered Individual Fact Checks

Individual student assessment might be indicated for students who have extreme difficulty with the cumulative Fact Checks. Using a set of fact cards, assess the child's fluency beginning with simpler facts and moving toward those that are causing difficulty. As a child misses, set the card aside. When a child misses five facts, stop and set a goal for those facts. Give the missed fact cards to the student, discuss any strategies that might help her better remember those facts, and determine a time frame for when you will recheck for mastery of the facts.

At times, you might want to conduct a more formal automaticity interview to gather further information on an individual student. For additional interview and note-taking ideas, see the Automaticity Interview form on the CD.

Connecting to Division

One Tiny Turtle, our Literature Link for multiplication, can also be used to teach division facts. After revisiting the original activity in which students built multiplication equations that represented the number of eggs in 1 nest, pose the following problem.

> A scientist found 7 eggs in 7 nests. Each nest had the same amount of eggs. How many eggs were in each nest?

Have students work with partners and draw 7 circles on a piece of paper to represent the 7 nests. Provide students with manipulatives to represent the 7 eggs and have them work together to solve the problem. After students have solved the problem, have students share how they solved it (see Figure 5.5). Display the equation $7 \div 7 = 1$, verbalizing that 7 eggs divided among 7 nests resulted in 1 egg in each nest. Provide students with several opportunities to absorb the ideas by changing the dividend and divisor of the problem (e.g., A scientist found 6 eggs in 6 nests or 3 eggs in 3 nests). Each time the new problem is solved by the students, be sure to connect it to the division equation. After a few problems have been solved, ask students to describe their observations about the division facts. Try questions like the following.

> *What changed in each division equation?*
>
> *What do you notice about the quotient of each problem?*
>
> *Do you think that every time we divide a number by itself the quotient will be 1? Why?*

Tip Mixed Fact Checks

The Mixed Fact Checks included on the CD contain new facts and previously learned facts to monitor both growth and retention. The first, third, and fifth columns on these checks assess new facts. The second and fourth columns assess previously learned facts.

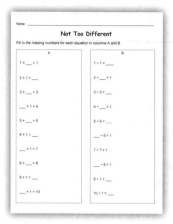

Figure 5.5 *This student drew 7 eggs and 7 nests (circles) and then crossed out each egg as he placed it in a nest.*

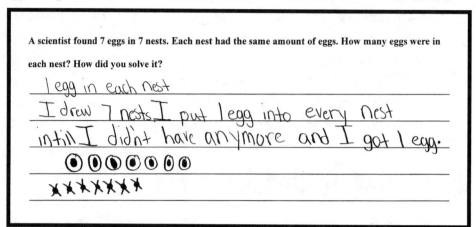

Students will soon recognize that the pattern in dividing a number by itself is similar to multiplying a number by 1. To reinforce this understanding, have students complete the activity *Not Too Different* (see CD). In this activity, students fill in missing numbers for a series of multiplication and division facts. After completing the equations, students explain how the two columns of facts are the same and how they are different.

CHAPTER SIX

Multiplying by 0

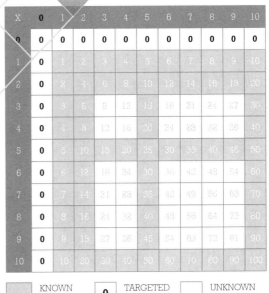

Students have now explored 1, 2, 5, and 10 as factors. 0 as a factor is similar to our exploration of ×1 facts in that it is easy in terms of automaticity but can present challenges in terms of understanding. Discussions of 0 groups and groups of 0 (yes, we know that 0 objects are not really a group!) will be important to promote understanding. On the other hand, a simple recognition that if either factor is 0 the product is 0 makes this the simplest fact for automaticity.

X	0	1	2	3	4	5	6	7	8	9	10
0	0	0	0	0	0	0	0	0	0	0	0
1	0	1	2	3	4	5	6	7	8	9	10
2	0	2	4	6	8	10	12	14	16	18	20
3	0	3	6	9	12	15	18	21	24	27	30
4	0	4	8	12	16	20	24	28	32	36	40
5	0	5	10	15	20	25	30	35	40	45	50
6	0	6	12	18	24	30	36	42	48	54	60
7	0	7	14	21	28	35	42	49	56	63	70
8	0	8	16	24	32	40	48	56	64	72	80
9	0	9	18	27	36	45	54	63	72	81	90
10	0	10	20	30	40	50	60	70	80	90	100

	KNOWN FACTS	**0**	TARGETED FACTS		UNKNOWN FACTS

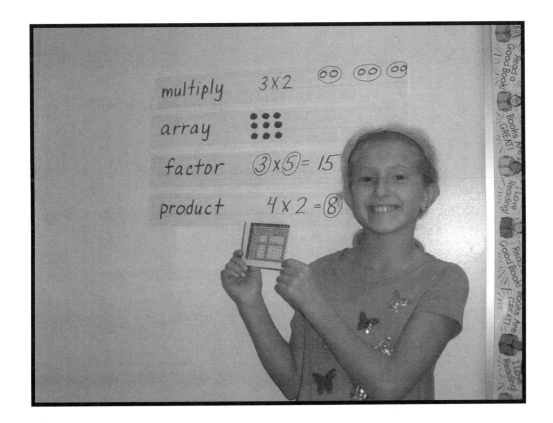

Focusing on the Big Ideas

When focusing on multiplication with 0 as a factor, some big ideas are:

If either factor is 0, the product will be 0.

This is known as the *zero property of multiplication*. This understanding is foundational. Rather than memorizing the property, we want to provide classroom experiences and discussions that help all students understand why this will always be true.

The order of the factors does not change the product (the commutative property).

Whether students are visualizing 0 groups of a certain size (e.g., 0×5 or 0 groups of 5) or whether they are visualizing groups of 0 (e.g., 5×0 or 5 groups of nothing), they notice that the products are always 0. The order does not matter.

These big ideas guide the types of questions we pose during class or small-group discussions.

What does it mean to multiply by 0?

What is a set of 0 items? Can you really have a group of 0?

What does it mean to have 0 sets?

When multiplying by 0, why would the product always be 0?

What patterns do you notice in the products?

Does the order of the factors affect the product? Give examples to justify your thinking.

Do you notice a connection between this multiplication equation and related division equation?

Our goal is to continually reinforce the big ideas related to math facts as we help students develop multiplication strategies.

Understanding ×0 Facts

Exploring the Facts: Problem Solving About School Supplies

Engaging students in hands-on explorations helps them make sense of 0 as a factor. The pattern that occurs with 0 as a factor is quite different from the patterns students have observed with 1, 2, 5, and 10 as factors. The product is always 0! Understanding multiplication with 0 makes mastering these facts a simple task.

Try an investigation with school supplies to review previously taught facts and introduce facts with 0 as a factor. Create 10 baskets of school supplies, each filled with 1 marker, 2 pencils, 5 crayons, and 10 paper clips. Place the 10 baskets in front of the class. Pose a few review problems for students to solve with partners, asking them to record a multiplication equation to solve each problem.

How many pencils are in 6 baskets? *6 × 2 = 12*

How many crayons are in 3 baskets? *3 × 5 = 15*

How many paper clips are in 9 baskets? *9 × 10 = 90*

How many markers are in 7 baskets? *7 × 1 = 7*

Have students report the multiplication equations and products as you review the factors they have already studied. Then, pose the following problem.

How many glue sticks are in 4 baskets?

Be prepared for possible confusion ("But there aren't any glue sticks!"). Have students share their ideas (see Figure 6.1). Discuss the way in which they recorded equations in the earlier problems. 6 baskets with 2 pencils in each basket is represented by the equation 6 × 2 = 12. How would they represent 4 baskets with 0 in each basket? After students have volunteered the idea, record 4 × 0 = 0.

Figure 6.1 *This student explains her reasoning for determining that there are no glue sticks.*

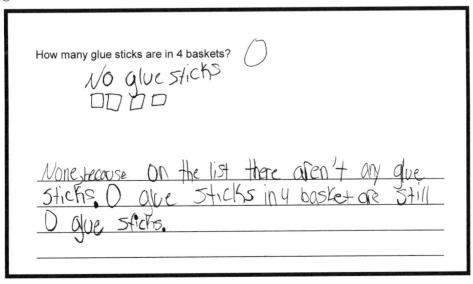

Work with students to begin a list of ×0 facts by observing the baskets. Select 1 basket and ask students how to record the number of glue sticks (*1 × 0 = 0*). Then select 2 baskets and again ask students how to record the number of glue sticks in 2 baskets (*2 × 0 = 0*). Ask students to work with partners to continue until they have recorded the facts from 1 to 10. Move through the room to check for student understanding or offer assistance. When partners have completed their fact lists, have them share their equations. Pose some problems like the following to determine if students have clearly understood the concept.

> If all of the baskets looked like these, how many glue sticks would be in 100 baskets? How do you know? How would we write the equation?

> If we had no baskets, how might we write the equation? Does 0 × 0 = 0 make sense? Why?

Literature Link: *Where the Wild Things Are*

In Maurice Sendak's *Where the Wild Things Are* (1988), Max sails to the land of the fearsome wild things and defeats them. This story sets the stage for conquering multiplication with 0.

Before Reading   Ask students to describe some physical features of monsters (e.g., horns, claws, teeth, wings, or webbed feet). Tell students that you will be reading a story about a little boy who visits an island filled with monsters. Tell them to observe the unusual features on the monsters in the story.

During Reading   While reading the story, stop occasionally to have students identify the physical features of the different monsters. Students may want to count the number of claws, ears, eyes, or teeth on some of the wild things. Make your pauses brief as students will want to hear the story events. You can further analyze the monsters after finishing the story.

After Reading   As a class, recall and describe the different wild things. Then, create a class monster on the board or on chart paper. Note the number of horns, eyes, ears, teeth, tails, legs, wings, or claws on your class monster. Ask the students to think-pair-share how many body parts there would be if the class created 2, 5, or 10 of your monster. As students share their ideas with the class, write equations on the board to identify the total number of each monster part.

Think-pair-share is a great way to engage all students.

1. Think about how many wings would be on 5 monsters. Don't raise your hand. Don't shout it out.

2. Tell your partner the total number of wings and how you figured it out.

3. Raise your hand and share your answer with the class.

Have the class identify a body part that your class monster does not have. Ask students to think about how many parts there would be altogether if you made 2, 5, or 10 of your monster (i.e., If the class monster is missing a tail, they would determine the number of tails for 2, 5, or 10 monsters). Students may look a bit confused, because there will be no tails on the monsters, no matter how many monsters you make. Ask students how they might write a multiplication equation to find the number of tails for 2 monsters with no tails (e.g., *2 × 0 = 0*). Record the equations for the number of tails on 5 and 10 tailless monsters, too.

After investigating the class monster, have students create their own monster (see *My Monster* activity on the CD) and list the number of different body parts on their monster. Make sure that they identify a body part that they did not include on their monster. Have students write equations to show the total number of parts if they created 6 monsters (see Figure 6.2). Students will enjoy a gallery walk (posting monsters around the room and walking the room to view them) to see the unique monsters made by their classmates.

Extend the lesson with some story-related problems for students to solve with partners.

> There were no oars on Max's ship. How many oars would be on 3 ships just like Max's? Explain how you know.

> There were no green monsters on the island. How many green monsters would be on 10 islands? Explain how you know.

Observe students as they discuss the problems with their partners to be sure they understand ×0 multiplication. Challenge students to work with partners to write a ×0 wild thing problem of their own.

Supporting All Learners
Posing Problems to Build Understanding
Problem-solving experiences build a stronger understanding of ×0 facts. Pose a variety of problems that represent ×0 situations and engage students in discussions about how

Figure 6.2 *This student shows her calculations and her creativity as she explores the number of body parts for 6 monsters.*

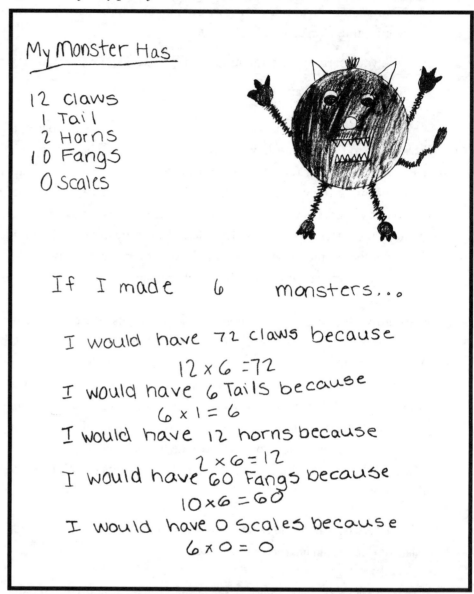

they determined the math fact that solved each problem. Try problems like the following.

> There were 4 plates on the table. There were no hamburgers on any of the plates. How many hamburgers were there? (4 × 0 = 0)

> There were 7 plates in the coin toss game at the carnival. There were no coins on any of the plates. How many coins were on the plates? (7 × 0 = 0)

Use problem-solving experiences and students' observations to help them generalize about ×0 facts. Try questions like:

Can you solve 25 × 0 = n? How do you know that your answer is correct?

Can you solve 25 × n = 0. How do you know that your answer is correct?

Challenge students to verbalize their thinking. Once they gain understanding of ×0 facts, memorizing them will be a breeze!

Exploring Misunderstandings As with multiplication with 1 as a factor, students' prior experiences with addition can lead to confusion when focusing on 0 as a factor. Adding 0 to any number will not change the sum, but multiplying by 0 results in a product of 0. Posting some addition and multiplication equations on the board and asking students to discuss ways in which they are alike and different is a good discussion starter.

$$0 \times 3 = 0 \qquad\qquad 0 + 3 = 3$$

Although the numbers in each equation are similar, attention must be paid to the symbols that indicate the appropriate operations. Circle the addition and multiplication symbols in the equations on the board. Provide students with a mix of addition and multiplication equations; have them circle the operation sign in each and then solve them.

When working with small groups, pose a multiplication or addition 0 fact and have students tell you the answer, or have each student write the answer on a small whiteboard. Emphasize the importance of not being *tricked* by the operation symbol.

Multiplying by 0 with Color Tiles or Cubes Remember the color tile activity from our exploration of ×1 facts in Chapter Five in which you filled 10 clear plastic bags with 1 green, 2 red, and 5 yellow tiles? Bring those bags back to clarify students' understanding of 0 facts! Pose questions to students about the total number of tiles in bags like the following:

How many yellow tiles are in 4 bags?

How many red tiles are in 7 bags?

How many blue tiles are in 5 bags?

Wait, there are no blue tiles in any of the bags!

Using a think-aloud technique supports many learners when they are confused by a math idea. The object of a think-aloud is to make our thinking visible to our students. We might say "But there aren't any blue tiles in the

5 bags! It's like there are 5 bags of 0 tiles. I think I'll put $5 \times 0 = 0$ because there are 5 bags, but there are 0 blue tiles in each bag and 0 blue tiles altogether." Recording the equations while talking aloud makes our thoughts even more visible to our students. Once we have modeled with our think-aloud, students can begin to build equations that represent the total number of blue tiles in 1–10 bags.

Building Automaticity

Targeted Practice

Students master ×0 facts quickly. Remind students that the product is 0 whenever 0 is a factor. This understanding makes automaticity with 0 a simple task.

Tip Capitalize on the minimal practice time needed for ×0 facts by including other fact sets in practice activities. Frequent review of previously learned math facts will increase students' fluency.

Creating and Storing Math Fact Games The initial effort to create each math fact game is well worth the hours of engaging practice it affords each student, and the templates on the CD make the creation of each game quite simple. For consumable game boards, on which students record scores, consider printing a stack to have on hand when needed. Other games do not require students to mark on the boards. For these games, consider printing the boards on card stock and laminating them so they can be used again and again. Parent volunteers might be enlisted to paste game boards and directions onto file folders or place them in manila envelopes to be used at classroom centers. Containers of number cubes, spinners, or game markers can be made available in plastic bins. Or consider storing both materials and game boards in plastic storage bags for use at centers or to send home for extra practice.

Zemory Cards		
0 × 5	5 × 0	0 × 3
Zemory	Zemory	Zemory
3 × 0	8 × 0	0 × 8
Zemory	Zemory	Zemory
0 × 9	9 × 0	2 × 7
Zemory	Zemory	Zemory
7 × 2	8 × 2	2 × 8
Zemory	Zemory	Zemory
5 × 9	9 × 5	9 × 10
Zemory	Zemory	Zemory
10 × 9	7 × 5	5 × 7
Zemory	Zemory	Zemory

Zemory Zemory is like the classic game of memory with a zero twist. In this game, students match fact cards based on the commutative property (e.g., if Liam flips a Zemory card that has 0×4 written on it, he looks for the 4×0 card to match). Partners take turns finding sets with matching factors and stating the product. The player with the most sets wins the game. Because ×0 facts are simple to remember, some previously learned fact pairs (e.g., 5×3, 3×5) are added to the game to provide review. And because the game cards are customizable, you can simply change the facts to ones that work best for your students.

Fact Sorting   Sorting activities are an engaging fact card review activity. Students are given assorted sets of fact cards (e.g., ×0, ×1, ×2, ×5, and ×10 facts) and asked to work with partners to sort the fact cards in a variety of ways. Some possibilities include:

- products that are 0 or products that are not 0

- products that are less than 20 or products that are greater than or equal to 20

- products that are even or products that are odd

Students receive repeated exposure to the facts as they work to sort their fact cards.

Monitoring Progress: Charting Foundation Facts

Finding ways for students to keep track of their progress as they master multiplication facts will give them a sense of accomplishment and will focus them on next steps. Provide students with a blank multiplication chart (see CD). After addressing the foundation facts (0, 1, 2, 5, 10) and providing students with repeated practice with those facts, have students record their known facts on their chart. Remind students of the commutative property to help them recognize their many known facts. Students will discover that eighty-five math facts are already known out of a total of 121 facts on a 0–10 multiplication chart (see Figure 6.3). That is more than two-thirds of their multiplication facts! With their understanding of the commutative property and their insights about patterns, they have built a strong foundation for the remaining thirty-six math facts. And they will quickly find that because of their understanding of the commutative property, there are actually only twenty-one math facts that still need to be memorized! Collect their charts or have them keep them in a safe place (i.e., glued inside the cover of a math journal) so they can add to them as they master more facts.

Tip   During fact card reviews, there is no need for a review with only ×0 fact cards, as the answer will always be 0. Blend the ×0 facts with other facts to require students to identify the ×0 facts as they appear in the mixed review.

Figure 6.3 *After recording their known facts, students realize that they are well on their way to math fact mastery.*

X	0	1	2	3	4	5	6	7	8	9	10
0	0	0	0	0	0	0	0	0	0	0	0
1	0	1	2	3	4	5	6	7	8	9	10
2	0	2	4	6	8	10	12	14	16	18	20
3	0	3	6			15					30
4	0	4	8			20					40
5	0	5	10	15	20	25	30	35	40	45	50
6	0	6	12			30					60
7	0	7	14			35					70
8	0	8	16			40					80
9	0	9	18			45					90
10	0	10	20	30	40	50	60	70	80	90	100

Connecting to Division

Division with 0 presents an opportunity to discuss students' understanding of the connection between multiplication and division.

$$30 \div 10 = 3 \text{ because } 3 \times 10 = 30$$
$$12 \div 2 = 6 \text{ because } 6 \times 2 = 12$$

We have told students to *think multiplication* when they see a division equation. What is $18 \div 2$? We tell students to think *what times 2 equals 18*. For $18 \div 2 = 9$ to be true, then $9 \times 2 = 18$ must also be true. We see this connection as we explore multiplication and division facts. Until we explore 0 facts!

To find quotients for 0 facts, students *think multiplication* as they have for previous facts, so to find the quotient for $0 \div 2$, they think *what times 2 equals 0* and, of course, $0 \times 2 = 0$. So whenever 0 is the dividend, the quotient will be 0 because any number multiplied by 0 will always be 0.

$0 \div 10 = 0$ because $0 \times 10 = 0$
$0 \div 4 = 0$ because $0 \times 4 = 0$

But what happens when 0 is the divisor? What about $2 \div 0$? Would the quotient be 0? If it was, then $0 \times 0 = 2$ and we know that is not true! Or students might ask themselves *what times 0 equals 2* and find that they have no answer. There is no number that will work as the quotient of $2 \div 0$ because 0 times any number is 0, not 2. So division by 0 doesn't work. Mathematicians call it *undefined*, which simply means there is no answer.

To prompt discussions and stimulate students' thinking, display a 0 fact family on the board and ask students to talk with partners to find the equation that does not make sense and to justify why.

$3 \times 0 = 0$ $0 \times 3 = 0$
$3 \div 0 = 0$ $0 \div 3 = 0$

Encourage students to *think multiplication* to determine that $3 \div 0 = 0$ does not make sense because $0 \times 0 \neq 3$.

Having these discussions helps students better understand the uniqueness of these division facts, but only 0 as a dividend is included in the Fact Checks.

CHAPTER SEVEN

Multiplying by 3

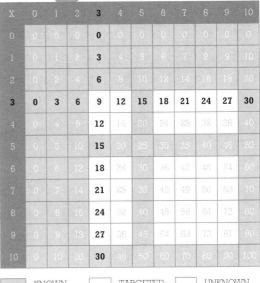

X	0	1	2	3	4	5	6	7	8	9	10
0	0	0	0	0	0	0	0	0	0	0	0
1	0	1	2	3	4	5	6	7	8	9	10
2	0	2	4	6	8	10	12	14	16	18	20
3	0	3	6	9	12	15	18	21	24	27	30
4	0	4	8	12	16	20	24	28	32	36	40
5	0	5	10	15	20	25	30	35	40	45	50
6	0	6	12	18	24	30	36	42	48	54	60
7	0	7	14	21	28	35	42	49	56	63	70
8	0	8	16	24	32	40	48	56	64	72	80
9	0	9	18	27	36	45	54	63	72	81	90
10	0	10	20	30	40	50	60	70	80	90	100

KNOWN FACTS   **3** TARGETED FACTS   UNKNOWN FACTS

Through their previous explorations with 0, 1, 2, 5, and 10 facts, our students have developed a strong foundation for the remaining math facts. They have had many opportunities to reflect on the concepts of multiplication and division. They have explored the commutative property in varied ways, and have committed a large set of math facts to memory. They are now ready to apply the knowledge and skills they have acquired to a new set of math facts. They are ready to explore facts with 3 as a factor.

Focusing on the Big Ideas

Big ideas form the backdrop for our math fact explorations. When focusing on multiplication with 3 as a factor, some big ideas include the following.

Multiplying by 3 is tripling a number.

Just as multiplying by 2 is doubling a number, multiplying by 3 is tripling a number. This can also be thought of as doubling the number and then adding 1 more set.

Our number system is a system of patterns.

Students will quickly see patterns in the ×3 facts, describing the pattern as skip-counting by 3, increasing each product by 3, or repeatedly adding 3.

The order of the factors does not change the product (the commutative property).

Whether students are visualizing 3 groups of a certain size (e.g., 3 × 5 or 3 groups of 5) or whether they are visualizing groups of 3 (e.g., 5 × 3 or 5 groups of 3), they understand that the products are the same.

These big ideas about numbers guide the types of questions we pose.

What does it mean to triple a number? How is it different from doubling a number?

What patterns do you notice in the products?

Does the order of the factors affect the product? Give examples to justify your thinking.

Do you notice a connection between this multiplication equation and related division equation?

Our goal is to continually reinforce the big ideas related to math facts as we help students develop multiplication strategies.

Understanding ×3 Facts

Literature Link: *A Three Hat Day*

A Three Hat Day by Laura Geringer (1985) is a fitting story to begin an exploration of ×3 facts. In this story, R. R. Pottle, a lonely man who loves hats, wears 2 hats when he is sad and 3 hats when he is very sad, and finally meets someone just like him.

Before Reading Begin by showing students the illustration on the cover of the book. Ask students to turn and talk with partners about why they think the man is wearing so many hats. Have partners share some of their ideas with the class. Ask students to listen to the story to find out why he is wearing so many hats.

During Reading While reading *A Three Hat Day*, be sure to show the illustrations so students can see R. R. Pottle's many hats.

After Reading Ask students why the man in the story wore so many hats. Ask students if it would be a good idea if everyone wore 2 hats when they were sad or 3 hats when they were really sad and to explain their thinking. Then, pose the following math problem:

> How many hats would we need if 4 people were feeling sad? How many hats would we need if 4 people were feeling very sad?

Have students work with partners to find the total number of hats for each situation. Provide students with connecting cubes so they can create stacks of 2 and 3 cubes to represent the stacks of 2 and 3 hats. With their previous knowledge of ×2 facts, students should not need to model that situation, but some might still like to check their answer with the physical model. Have the class share their solutions. Ask students to turn and tell a partner the multiplication equations to go with the problem (e.g., $4 \times 2 = 8$ for 4 people with 2 hats and $4 \times 3 = 12$ for 4 people with 3 hats).

Acknowledge that most people wear only 1 hat at a time, but that the quirky character in the story had 2-hat days and 3-hat days. Tell students they will be writing multiplication equations for 1-, 2-, and 3-hat days. Model the first one together as you ask them how many hats 1 person would wear on a 1-hat day. Record *$1 \times 1 = 1$* on the board as you verbalize "1 man wearing 1 hat is 1 total hat." Continue by asking how many hats 1 person would wear on a 2-hat day and record *$1 \times 2 = 2$* just below the first equation, stating "1 man wearing 2 hats is 2 total hats." Finally, discuss the number of hats 1 person would wear on a 3-hat day and record *$1 \times 3 = 3$* below the other two equations, stating "1 man wearing 3 hats is 3 total hats." Ask students to work with partners to write the equations to show 1-, 2-, and 3-hat days for 2–10 people. Remind them that they already know the ×1 and ×2 math facts, but they may use their cubes to determine the number of hats for the 3-hat days.

After partners have completed their equations for 1-, 2-, and 3-hat days, check for accurate answers. Then, ask partners to discuss patterns in the math facts.

How are the ×1, ×2, and ×3 facts alike? How are they different?

How do the ×3 facts compare to the ×1 facts? (triple the amount)

How do the ×3 facts compare to the ×2 facts? (have one more set)

Have students use their connecting cubes to test some of their conjectures (see Figure 7.1). Have them select a number of people (e.g., 6 people) and show a stack of cubes to represent the total number of hats on a 1-hat day (6 hats), a 2-hat day (12 hats), and a 3-hat day (18 hats). Have students compare their stacks of connecting cubes. What do they notice? Have them try it with a few more examples to see if the relationship between the stacks will always be the same.

Finally, have students summarize their insights about ×3 facts, verbally or in writing, as you record some of their ideas on the board.

Tip Recording sheets are provided on the CD for many of the math fact activities, but students can easily record activity data in their math journals in a less formal format.

Figure 7.1 *Partners use linking cubes to visualize and compare 1 × 6, 2 × 6, and 3 × 6.*

Exploring the Facts: Doubling and Tripling Baskets of Fruit

Explore the concept of triples, beginning with a review of doubles, by posing the following problem.

> The Franklin Zoo has some very special animals that attract lots of visitors each day. There are twin apes, Brady and Grady, and a set of chimpanzee triplets, Barry, Larry, and Jerry. One day, the zookeeper brought them each a basket of their favorite fruits. Each basket held the following:
>
> 1 grapefruit
>
> 2 peaches
>
> 3 oranges
>
> 4 apples
>
> 5 lemons
>
> 6 bananas
>
> 7 strawberries
>
> 8 raspberries
>
> 9 grapes
>
> 10 blueberries
>
> How many of each fruit will the zookeeper need in order to create fruit baskets for the twin apes?

Remind students that they will need to double the quantity of each fruit since there are 2 apes. Have students work with partners and record the amounts for each fruit on the *Fruit Baskets* recording sheet (see CD). Move through the room to monitor their work, checking for students who are using their understanding of ×2 facts to quickly find the solutions. Record the class findings on the board.

Next, have students work with partners to determine the amount of fruit the zookeeper will need in order to fill the 3 fruit baskets for the chimpanzee triplets. Have a basket of counters available for students who need a hands-on approach for determining the amounts. Have students record their answers on the appropriate column of the recording sheet. Begin a class discussion, and record the solutions for the chimpanzee triplets next to the solutions for the ape twins on the board.

Challenge partners to observe the recorded amounts and record any patterns or insights about the numbers on their charts. Engage students in a class

Tip **Thinking About Numbers**

Help students make sense of math facts and enhance their number sense by asking them to observe and discuss their data for all 5 primates (2 apes and 3 chimpanzees). How does the sum of the ×2 and ×3 columns compare with the ×5 product? Can students verbalize why they are the same?

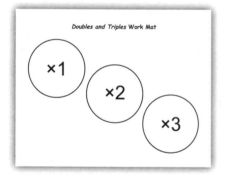

Doubles and Triples Work Mat

×1 ×2 ×3

0–99 Chart

0	1	2	3	4	5	6	7	8	9
10	11	12	13	14	15	16	17	18	19
20	21	22	23	24	25	26	27	28	29
30	31	32	33	34	35	36	37	38	39
40	41	42	43	44	45	46	47	48	49
50	51	52	53	54	55	56	57	58	59
60	61	62	63	64	65	66	67	68	69
70	71	72	73	74	75	76	77	78	79
80	81	82	83	84	85	86	87	88	89
90	91	92	93	94	95	96	97	98	99

discussion about the patterns (e.g., vertical pattern of skip counting by twos or adding 2 in the doubles column; pattern of skip-counting by 3 or adding 3 in the triples column). Explore connections between the columns as you have students explore the numbers in each row. Do students notice that triples are like doubles with 1 more set added? Could students find a triples amount if they knew the double? If the double is 10, what would the triple be? Why? If the double is 20, what would the triple be? Why?

Supporting All Learners

Some students may benefit from additional explorations with ×3 facts. Following are a variety of activities to strengthen their understanding and fluency.

Visualizing Doubles and Triples   Provide each student with a set of counters and a Doubles and Triples Work Mat (see CD). Have students select 2 counters and place them in the first circle on their mat. Write *2* on the board. Ask them to place double the amount in the ×2 circle on their mat (e.g., 4 counters). Record *2 × 2 = 4* on the board. Point to the original 2 on the board. Ask students how many they would have if they tripled that amount. Ask questions to be sure students know what *tripling* means (e.g., 3 times as much or multiplying by 3). Have them place 3 times as many counters in the ×3 circle on their mat (e.g., 6 counters). Ask them to observe the counters in the 3 groups and share their observations. How many more are in the second circle than the first? How many more are in the third circle than the second? If they know ×2, how might they find ×3? Repeat the process with other numbers to build students' understanding that multiplying by 3 will result in 1 more group than multiplying by 2.

Visualizing Patterns   Explore patterns by having students color in multiples of 3 on a 0–99 chart (see the CD). Have students begin by verbalizing as they multiply 3 × 0 = 0 (then color the 0), 3 × 1 = 3 (then color the 3). Have students continue to 3 × 10 = 30 (color the 30). Ask students to stop and observe the multiples they have colored. What pattern do they see? Can they predict the next multiples? Have them use calculators to check if their predictions are correct as they complete the 0–99 chart.

Multiplying by 3 with Connected Cubes   Explore scenarios with 3 as a factor by using sets of 3 connected cubes. Provide students with a basket of cubes and have them create 10 chains of 3 cubes each. Then, as a math fact is posed (e.g., 5 × 3), have students select the appropriate number of chains (5 chains of 3 cubes) and determine the total number of cubes. Students can continue the activity with partners by spinning a number 1–10, multiplying that number by 3, and then drawing the chains and recording the appropriate equation on blank paper or on the *Multiplication Chains* recording sheet on the CD. The student in Figure 7.2 shows how she determined the total number of cubes in 5 chains.

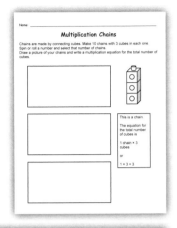

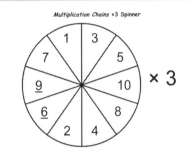

What Comes in Threes?   Help students visualize ×3 facts by connecting them to real-world examples. Ask students to turn and share things that come in threes (e.g., wheels on a tricycle, angles on a triangle, colors on a street light). Pose problems about the real-world threes (i.e., How many wheels on 4 tricycles? How many angles on 5 triangles? How many colors on 6 street lights?). Challenge high-level learners with more complex data (i.e., How many wheels on a dozen tricycles?).

Creating Folded Books or Three-Column Charts   Writing about math ideas helps students process their ideas and allows us to assess their understanding. Make writing fun for your students by asking them to fold a paper into thirds to create a folded book about multiplying by 3 or simply provide them with a three-column chart (see CD). Have students select a ×3 fact. In one section, have students write a word problem that goes with their fact. In the next section, have them draw an array or picture that shows the math fact. In the third section, have them share a tip for multiplying by 3. Have them record the math fact, along with the product, on the front of their folded book or on the top of their three-column chart (see Figure 7.3).

Figure 7.2 *Following a hands-on exploration, this student draws a representation and creates an equation to match the math fact.*

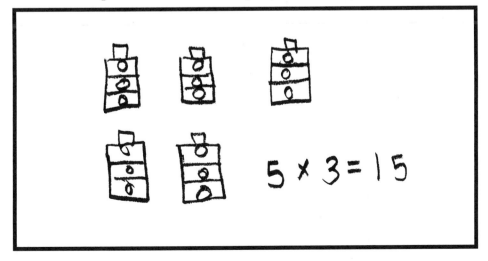

Figure 7.3 *This student shows his understanding of 4 × 3 in varied ways.*

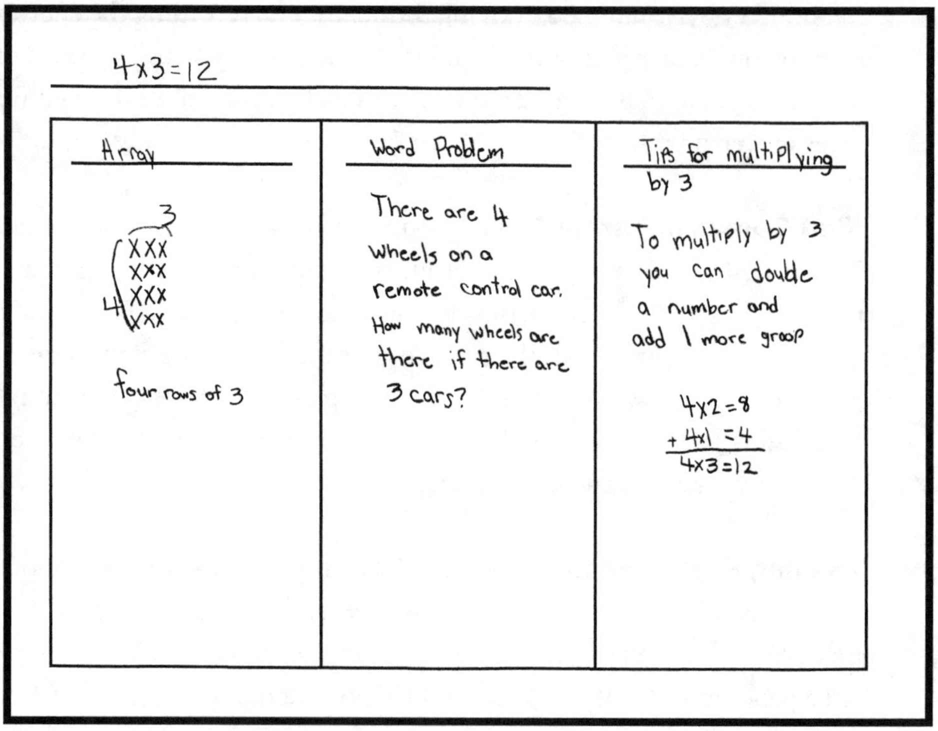

Building Automaticity

Targeted Practice

After students have engaged in a variety of activities to understand multiplication with 3 as a factor, it is time to provide them with repeated opportunities to practice the facts.

Integrating Writing into Practice Experiences   Writing prompts that encourage students to express their math ideas are a great addition to math fact games. After playing the game, students might be asked:

How did this game help you with your math facts?

If you didn't know the facts in this game, what strategy could you use to help you find the products?

What strategy did you use to play this game?

What facts will you review before you play this game again?

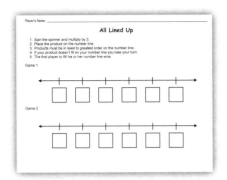

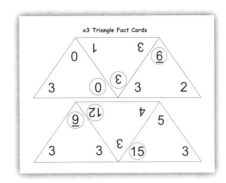

All Lined Up   *All Lined Up* is a strategy game that helps students with ×3 facts and number relationships. Each player has a number line game board with six empty boxes. Players take turns spinning numbers and multiplying by 3. They then place their product in one of the six empty boxes; however, the numbers must be placed in correct sequence (i.e., if a player has 3, 9, and 15 in her first three boxes and spins a 12 on her next turn, she cannot play the 12 and loses her turn). The first player to fill all six boxes wins.

Triangle Fact Cards to Review ×3 Facts

Triangle fact cards (see template on CD) provide a great opportunity to reinforce the connection between multiplication and division facts and to work toward mastery of both. The three angles of the triangle hold the two factors and the product for a given fact. The product is circled. As the teacher (or a partner) covers one corner, the student must either name the product (if both factors are visible) or the missing factor (if a factor and product are visible). Triangle fact cards can be used for partner practice, home practice, or for a teacher-led small-group review. Additional triangle fact card activities include:

- Provide students with blank triangles and have them create their own set of triangle fact cards for the ×3 facts.

- Provide students with ×3 fact cards. As they select a card, they must write the four multiplication/division equations represented by the card (fact families).

Monitoring Progress: Individual Student Conferences

Taking the time to confer with individual students allows you to assess their progress and focus them on specific goals. As your students are engaged in practice tasks or visiting math centers, invite individual students to meet with you to review their most recent Fact Check. Examine blank or incorrect math facts. Ask students which facts are difficult for them to remember. Provide tips and reminders to help them master those facts. Record a few unknown

 Modifying Activities from Previous Chapters

Remember that activities from previous chapters can be easily adapted for ×3 facts. You might want to adapt the following for ×3 fact reviews:

Fact Card Jumps (Chapter Two)

Fact Grids (Chapter Three)

Fact Card Arrays (Chapter Four)

Fact Sorting (Chapter Six)

facts on index cards and give the cards to the student to take home for practice. Praise each student for the facts he does know and encourage each student to continue reviewing the unknown facts.

Connecting to Division

Activities that connect multiplication and division help strengthen students' understanding of the link between these concepts. Using the familiar context from the *Baskets of Fruit* exploration activity, but modifying the situation to represent a division scenario, will provide practice with division facts and bolster understanding of the link between the operations. Pose the following problem.

> The zookeeper sent his assistant to the store to buy fruit for the chimpanzee triplets, Barry, Larry, and Jerry. He bought 3 grapefruit, 6 peaches, 9 oranges, 12 apples, 15 lemons, 18 bananas, 21 strawberries, 24 raspberries, 27 grapes, and 30 blueberries. How will the zookeeper figure out how many of each type of fruit should go in each basket?

Remind students that the zookeeper wants to be sure that each chimpanzee gets the same amount of each type of fruit. Have students talk with a partner to brainstorm how they will figure out the solution. Have them share their ideas, being sure to highlight the operation of division as a way to determine the fair share for each chimpanzee.

Have students work with partners to select 3 different kinds of fruit, determine the quantity each chimpanzee will get, draw pictures to show the 3 groups, and record their division equations (Figure 7.4). Have counters available for students who would benefit from using them. When partners have determined their solutions, have them share their ideas as you record the division equations on the board. As you record the equations, highlight the 3 equal groups by using pictures or concrete materials to visually check the solutions.

Triangle Fact Cards

Triangle fact cards, mentioned earlier for practice with multiplication facts, are a perfect tool for also practicing division. Simply cover one of the factors on the card, so students see the product and remaining factor, and the cards become a division practice activity.

Figure 7.4 *This student shows her understanding of division through drawings and equations to represent each situation.*

Baskets of Fruit

The zookeeper sent his assistant to the store to buy fruit for the chimpanzee triplets, Barry, Larry, and Jerry. He bought 3 grapefruit, 6 peaches, 9 oranges, 12 apples, 15 lemons, 18 bananas, 21 strawberries, 24 raspberries, 27 grapes, and 30 blueberries. Choose three different fruits. Draw a picture and write an equation to tell how much fruit each chimpanzee gets.

Fruit	Picture	Equation
6 peaches		$6 \div 3 = 2$
15 lemons	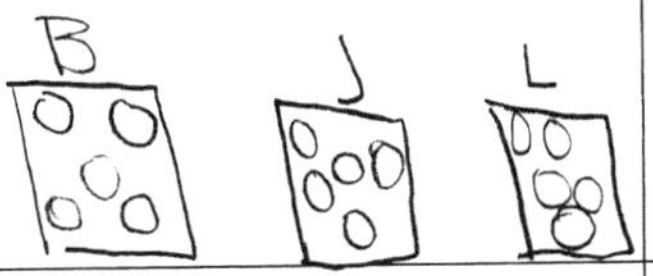	$15 \div 3 = 5$
30 blue-berries	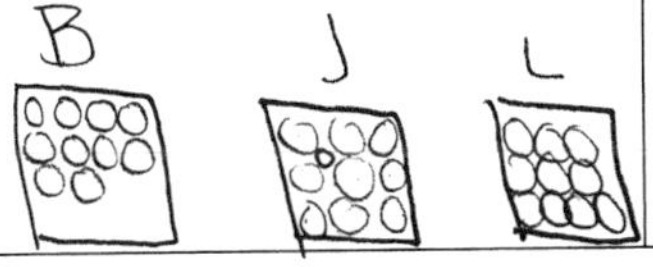	$30 \div 3 = 10$

CHAPTER EIGHT

Multiplying by 4

We began our study of math facts by focusing on facts with 2 as a factor. Our students have had ongoing opportunities to explore these facts and practice for fluency. As we begin a study of ×4 facts, we capitalize on students' understanding and mastery of ×2 facts to provide the foundation for mastering this new set of facts.

X	0	1	2	3	4	5	6	7	8	9	10
0	0	0	0	0	0	0	0	0	0	0	0
1	0	1	2	3	4	5	6	7	8	9	10
2	0	2	4	6	8	10	12	14	16	18	20
3	0	3	6	9	12	15	18	21	24	27	30
4	0	4	8	12	16	20	24	28	32	36	40
5	0	5	10	15	20	25	30	35	40	45	50
6	0	6	12	18	24	30	36	42	48	54	60
7	0	7	14	21	28	35	42	49	56	63	70
8	0	8	16	24	32	40	48	56	64	72	80
9	0	9	18	27	36	45	54	63	72	81	90
10	0	10	20	30	40	50	60	70	80	90	100

KNOWN FACTS   **4** TARGETED FACTS   UNKNOWN FACTS

Focusing on the Big Ideas

By focusing on big ideas about mathematics during our teaching of math facts, we strengthen students' understanding of numbers. When focusing on multiplication with 4 as a factor, the following are big ideas.

Multiplication by 4 is doubling a double.

Students have already explored doubling when they investigated ×2 facts. Multiplying by 4 is simply doubling the product of the ×2 fact.

Our number system is a system of patterns.

Noticing that multiples of 4 are always even numbers or realizing that multiples of 4 are also multiples of 2 (in fact, that they are every other multiple of 2) leads to interesting conversation and insights.

The order of the factors does not change the product (the commutative property).

As with all other facts students have studied, they recognize that the order of the factors will not change the product. Based on this understanding, students realize that they already know many of the ×4 facts because they have already studied factors of 0, 1, 2, 3, 5, and 10.

Key questions related to the big ideas for ×4 facts:

What does it mean to have twice as much? What does it mean to double a quantity?

What does it mean to double a double?

What patterns do you notice in the products?

Does the order of the factors affect the product? Give examples to justify your thinking.

Are all multiples of 4 also multiples of 2? Why?

Which multiples of 2 are also multiples of 4? Why?

Are multiples of 4 always even numbers? Why?

Tip The concept of doubling continues to be a critical understanding as students see the connection between the newly introduced ×4 facts and the previously learned ×2 facts.

Our goal is to continually reinforce the big ideas related to math facts as we help students develop multiplication strategies.

Understanding ×4 Facts

Literature Link: *If You Hopped Like a Frog*

In *If You Hopped Like a Frog*, David Schwartz (2000) shares amazing feats people could achieve if they had the abilities of various animals and insects. Schwartz highlights the jumping ability of frogs, the speed of spiders, the strength of ants, and many other fun animal to human comparisons.

Before Reading   Ask students if they have ever thought about being an animal. Read the letter from the author at the beginning of the book in which the author talks about wishing he was a frog and other animals. Have students turn to a partner and share an animal or insect they might like to be and why.

During Reading   Read the story once to have fun with the animal to human comparisons. Then reread the story, this time asking students to think about the number of legs for the different animals and insects as you read. Have students create a line plot on their paper as you create one on the board, labeling it with numbers 0–8 for the number of legs for each animal mentioned. As each animal or insect is mentioned, ask students to share the number of legs and then place an *X* on the corresponding number on their line plot as you record it on your line plot (see Figure 8.1).

Ask students to turn and tell a partner what their line plot shows about the animal legs. You might ask them to identify the fewest legs and the most legs that any animal or insect had in the story. You might ask them which quantity of legs was mentioned most often. You might explore which types of animals or insects had various quantities of legs (e.g., insects, spiders, humans, birds).

Figure 8.1 *This line plot shows the number of legs for the animals in the story.*

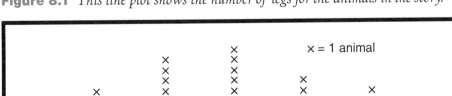

After Reading   Have students identify the number of legs that most animals had in the story (4) and compare that number to the number of legs people have (2). Begin posing questions about animal legs and people legs (i.e., How many legs would 6 people have? How many legs would 6 frogs have?). Have students first predict the number of legs for 6 frogs and 6 humans. Have them turn and tell a partner their prediction and how they determined the prediction. Then, ask students to draw a diagram for each situation and write a multiplication sentence to show the actual number of legs (e.g., 6 × 2 = 12 and 6 × 4 = 24).

With the class, make a list of the 4-legged animals from the story (e.g., frog, brachiosaurus, shrew, chameleon, bear). Have students choose a 4-legged animal from the list. Using the *How Many Legs?* recording sheet (see template on CD), have students select a number card from a deck of 2–10 number cards (see CD template) and place that number on the Number of People or Animals line on the recording sheet. Students draw a diagram and write a multiplication equation to find the amount of legs for that quantity of people, and then do the same to find the amount of legs for that quantity of animals. Remind students that they do not need to draw animals, but might use circles, *X*s, or tallies). Have students repeat the process by randomly picking another number card from the 2–10 deck to indicate a new quantity of humans and animals.

After students have determined the total number of legs for two different-sized animal/human groups, have them share their data as you record it on the board. Chart the ×2 multiplication equations in one column and the ×4 in another column, progressing in order from 2–10 animals or humans in a group. As you record the data gathered by the class, have each student record the data on a paper folded into two columns or on the *Exploring Legs* recording sheet on the CD. Have students turn to partners and compare the products of the multiplication equations. Jump-start their thinking with some questions.

> *What do you notice about the data?*
>
> *How are the ×2 and ×4 facts related?*
>
> *How might this help you remember the ×4 facts?*

Have students work with partners to write about their observations (see Figure 8.2).

Figure 8.2 *This student recognizes that knowing ×2 facts can help her find ×4 facts.*

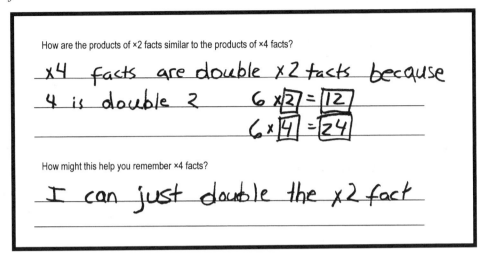

How are the products of ×2 facts similar to the products of ×4 facts?

x4 facts are double x2 facts because
4 is double 2   6 x 2 = 12
                 6 x 4 = 24

How might this help you remember ×4 facts?

I can just double the x2 fact

Exploring the Facts: Visualizing Patterns on a 1–40 Chart

Explore patterns by having students chart multiples of 2 and 4 on a 1–40 chart (see the template on the CD). First, ask students to locate the multiples of two on the chart, circling each one. Next, have students place an *X* on all multiples of 4. Have students work with partners to record their observations as they look at their completed 1–40 chart (see Figure 8.3), then have them share their ideas with the whole class.

Figure 8.3 *The 1–40 chart allows students to identify connections between the two sets of math facts.*

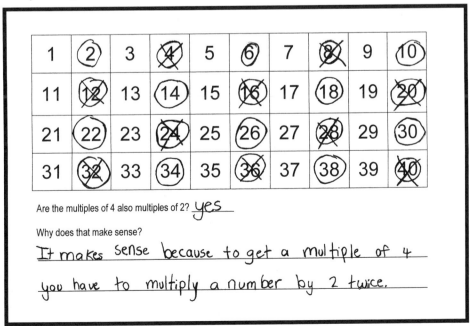

Are the multiples of 4 also multiples of 2? yes

Why does that make sense?

It makes sense because to get a multiple of 4 you have to multiply a number by 2 twice.

Are multiples of 4 also multiples of 2? Does that make sense? Why?

Is every other multiple of 2 also a multiple of 4? Does that make sense? Why?

Are all multiples of 4 even numbers? Does that make sense? Why?

Record their insights on chart paper as you discuss their observations and explanations. Ask them to share how understanding these patterns might help them find the answers to ×4 facts.

Supporting All Learners

Following are some additional activities that may be done with the whole class, but may also be perfect for small teacher-led groups of students who need additional exposure to the concepts.

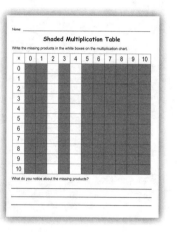

Observing Patterns with Shaded Multiplication Tables Provide each student with a shaded multiplication table (see the template on the CD). Have students fill the open sections of their shaded table by recording the multiples of 2 and the multiples of 4. Once students have filled the blanks, have them work with partners to check their answers. If partners do not agree on the products, have students raise their hands for your assistance. If they agree on the products, ask them to examine the facts, looking for patterns and connections between the numbers, and to record their observations. Once students have recorded observations, guide them in a discussion to focus on the patterns they have noticed. Observations will likely include:

The 2 facts are like counting by 2 or repeatedly adding 2.

The 4 facts are like counting by 4 or repeatedly adding 4.

The 2 facts are even numbers.

The 4 facts are even numbers but every other even number.

The 4 facts are twice as much as the corresponding 2 facts.

Notice how these observations relate to the big ideas discussed earlier in the chapter. Observing math facts and attempting to explain their observations provides a rich exploration into numbers and number properties and results in a better understanding of the math facts. Shaded multiplication tables allow students to focus on specific rows of facts (or columns depending on how you choose to shade the table) and support students who may become overwhelmed by the quantity of numbers on a full multiplication table.

Animal Models to Find Products For students who need to see the ×4 facts in a very concrete way, gather some plastic animal models (e.g., bears, dinosaurs, farm animals) from a dollar store or toy store. Be sure to remove any animals that do not have 4 legs. Allow students to group the animals in groups of 1–10 and then explore and record the total number of legs for each group (i.e., making a group of 4 bears and determining that there are 16 total legs). Students might count, skip-count, or add to find the total, but be sure to consistently talk about the multiplication process by noting that 4 bears with 4 legs have $4 \times 4 = 16$ legs. This activity is a nice way to follow the *If You Hopped Like a Frog* activity earlier in this chapter and provides a hands-on version of that activity for concrete thinkers.

Capitalizing on Real-World Connections Real-world examples help students visualize math ideas. Prompt students to brainstorm real things that come in fours. Some possibilities include:

- 4 legs on a table or chair
- 4 wheels on a wagon
- 4 horseshoes on a horse
- 4 feet on a mouse

Pose some ×4 problems using their real-world examples. Problems might include:

How many legs are on 5 tables?

How many wheels are on 8 wagons?

How many horseshoes are on 6 horses?

Allow students to use manipulatives or draw pictures as they initially explore the ×4 facts.

Tip Students benefit from hands-on experiences as they work to make sense of math facts.

Building Automaticity

Targeted Practice

Once students understand the concept of ×4, it is time to provide repeated opportunities for them to practice the facts.

Games for At-Home Play Parents are often willing but unsure how to help their children at home. Math fact games provide parents with specific activities that support their children's math skills and provide for fun family time. Before sending games home, be sure that your students have played the game in school and understand how it is played. Providing written directions is helpful. Students might sign out game materials from a lending library (e.g., bags filled with directions, game board, number cube, or other needed materials) or you might simply send home directions for playing simple games requiring only their math fact cards or a deck of playing cards. See the CD for a letter inviting parents to play math fact games with their children. The letter includes tips for at-home play and is customizable so you can add your own ideas.

Fact Fish *Fact Fish* is much like the traditional game of *Go Fish*. Players are dealt 12 cards (see CD for *Fact Fish* ×4 cards). The players then take turns making ×4 fact sets. A set includes both factors and a product. For example, Susie would make a set with a 3, a 4, and a 12 because $3 \times 4 = 12$. Each fact set must have a *4* as a factor, because our focus is on practicing ×4 facts.

During a turn, one player asks another player for a specific card. If the opponent has the card, the player collects it and makes a set. If the opponent doesn't have the card, the player must fish for a card (pull the next card from the pile) and discard one card. The maximum number of cards a player can have is twelve. The first player to make three sets wins.

Crisscross Facts For hands-on fact practice, provide students with a set of ×4 fact cards and a set of 40 flat sticks (e.g., flat coffee stirrers or $11 \times \frac{1}{2}$-inch strips cut from card stock). Have students select a fact card (e.g., 4×3) and represent the fact by placing 4 sticks vertically and then laying 3 sticks on top of them horizontally (see Figure 8.4). Students then find the product by counting the 12 intersections of the sticks. Students record the multiplication equation, then choose a new fact card and begin again.

Figure 8.4 *Crossing sticks provides a hands-on exploration of facts.*

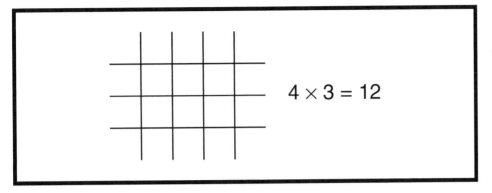

$4 \times 3 = 12$

◆ **Tip** **Modifying Activities from Previous Chapters**

Remember that activities from previous chapters can be easily adapted for ×4 facts. You might want to try:

Fact Card Jumps (Chapter Two)

Fact Card Arrays (Chapter Four)

Fact Sorting (Chapter Six)

Triangle Fact Cards (Chapter Seven)

Multi-Models In *Multi-Models*, students practice facts while drawing area models of the facts. Players begin with a blank grid (see CD template). One player begins by pulling a ×4 fact card from a facedown deck. That player then outlines an area model representation of the fact on his grid, labeling it with the fact (see Figure 8.5). Players take turns pulling cards and drawing area models until a player cannot fit a model on his grid for three consecutive turns. The player who is able to fit the most models on his grid wins.

Altering Fact Card Sets to Provide Specific Reviews As mentioned in previous chapters, fact cards can be used for a variety of practice activities from partner reviews to sorting tasks to drawing arrays. Fact cards might be used to review one set of facts (e.g., cards for just the ×4 facts) or might be used to review previously learned facts. As students become more skilled, re-moving some of the facts that have already been mastered (e.g., 0, 1, 2) will provide more repetition of the facts that still need work.

Monitoring Progress: Progress Graphs

Each time students complete a Fact Check for a specific set of facts (e.g., ×4 facts), have them add their data to their own progress graph. This simple bar graph (see CD template) allows students to record the number of facts correct on each Fact Check and documents their progress.

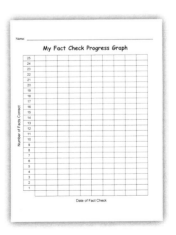

Figure 8.5 *This game reinforces the concept of area as well as offering math facts practice.*

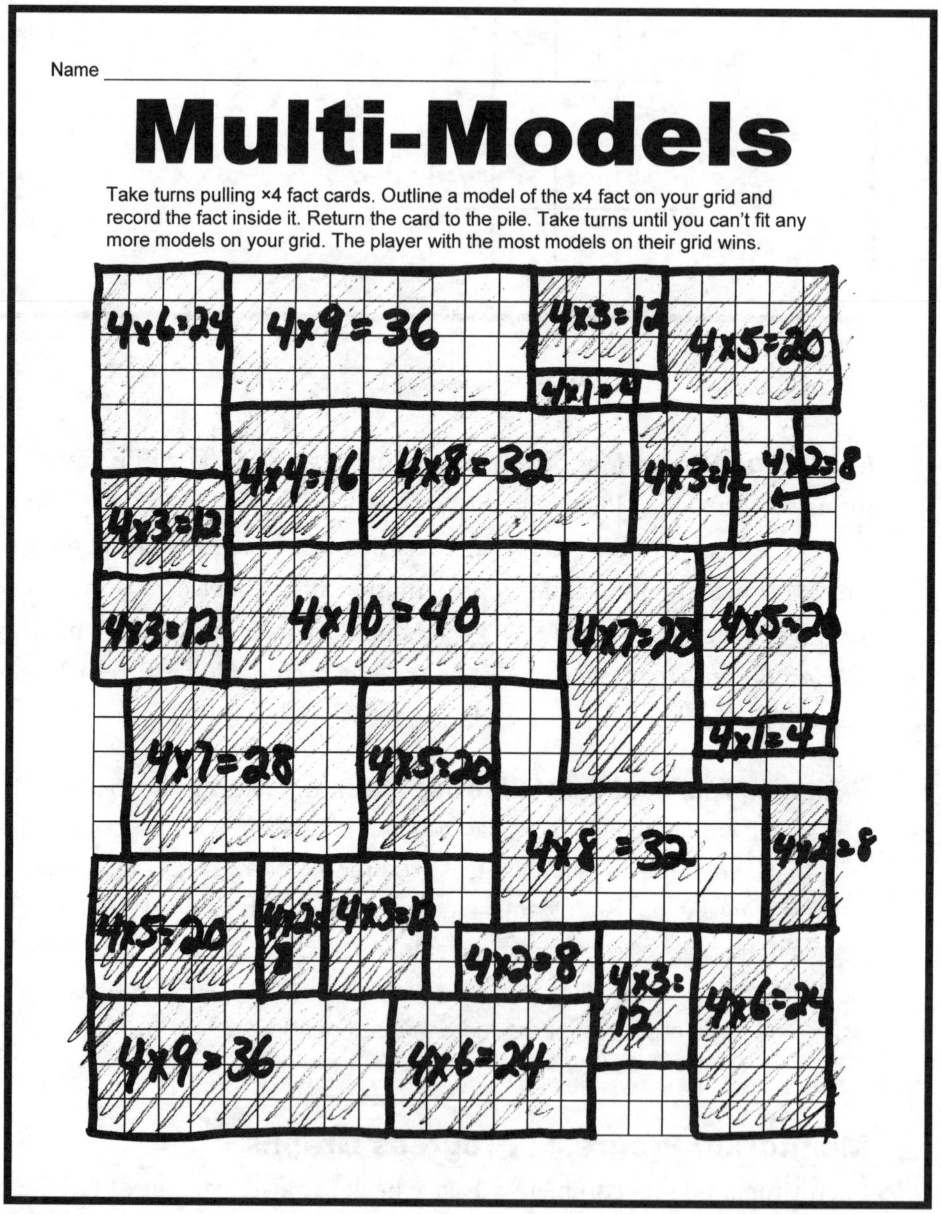
Name ______________________________

Multi-Models

Take turns pulling ×4 fact cards. Outline a model of the x4 fact on your grid and record the fact inside it. Return the card to the pile. Take turns until you can't fit any more models on your grid. The player with the most models on their grid wins.

Comparing a student's performance on a Fact Check to her own prior performance with that set of facts is the most productive comparison. Comparing students to other, more successful students leads to increased frustration and anxiety. Students master math facts at different rates. It is our goal to find activities to support all levels of learners as they work to master these facts, as well as to continue to motivate and engage our struggling students. Celebrating progress is a critical factor in motivating students to continue working toward automaticity.

Connecting to Division

As students develop an understanding of multiplication with 4 as a factor, take every opportunity to talk about the connection between multiplication and division facts. Problem situations that focus on animals are an ideal context to explore division concepts. Try some problems like these:

> There are 24 legs. How many dogs are there?

> There are 36 legs. How many turtles are there?

> There are 32 legs. How many polar bears are there?

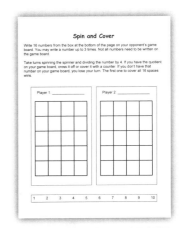

Have students record the division equations as they solve each animal problem. Providing them with counters or cubes to represent the legs will support those students who need to physically solve each problem.

Challenge students to write some animal division problems of their own. Have them write the word problem and record the division equation that solves their problem.

Spin and Cover

In *Spin and Cover* (see CD), players attempt to cover all of the quotients on their game board. The twist in this game is that players write the quotients on their opponent's game boards. Players can write the same quotient up to three times. Players then take turns spinning and saying the quotient. If the quotient is on her game board, the player crosses it off. Only one quotient can be crossed off with each spin. If a quotient is not on the game board, the player loses her turn. The first player to cross off all of her quotients wins.

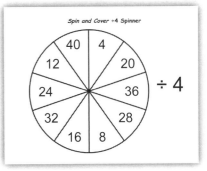

CHAPTER NINE

Multiplying by 6

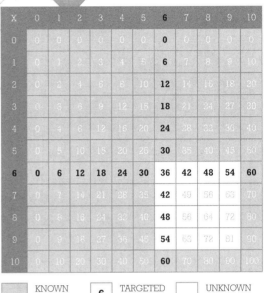

Linking new ideas to previously learned concepts allows students to better grasp the new ideas. A strategic way to explore multiplication with 6 as a factor is to build on students' previous mastery of ×3 facts and explore the connection between ×3 and ×6 facts. The concept of doubling threes to find the product for sixes provides a natural foundation for mastery of the ×6 facts. In addition, students' mastery of ×5 facts aids their understanding of ×6 facts. Knowing the product for 5 groups of a

X	0	1	2	3	4	5	6	7	8	9	10
0	0	0	0	0	0	0	**0**	0	0	0	0
1	0	1	2	3	4	5	**6**	7	8	9	10
2	0	2	4	6	8	10	**12**	14	16	18	20
3	0	3	6	9	12	15	**18**	21	24	27	30
4	0	4	8	12	16	20	**24**	28	32	36	40
5	0	5	10	15	20	25	**30**	35	40	45	50
6	**0**	**6**	**12**	**18**	**24**	**30**	**36**	**42**	**48**	**54**	**60**
7	0	7	14	21	28	35	**42**	49	56	63	70
8	0	8	16	24	32	40	**48**	56	64	72	80
9	0	9	18	27	36	45	**54**	63	72	81	90
10	0	10	20	30	40	50	**60**	70	80	90	100

KNOWN FACTS | **6** TARGETED FACTS | UNKNOWN FACTS

certain size helps students identify the product if 1 more group is added. And students who understand the concept of tripling may notice the connection between ×2 and ×6 facts. The more students build their understanding of the many connections between math facts, the more each set of facts makes sense to them.

Focusing on the Big Ideas

Exploring big ideas about mathematics provides the backdrop for our exploration of 6 as a factor. Following are some big ideas for ×6 facts.

In multiplication, if we double the number of sets or double the size of each set, the product will double.

This, of course, does not hold true if 0 is the factor, because we can't really double 0! Students have already explored the effect of doubling a factor when they investigated the connection between ×2 and ×4 facts. Now, they experience it again as they explore the connection between ×3 and ×6 facts. Students might even notice the tripling connection as they observe ×2 and ×6 facts. Observing these connections between math facts helps build strong number sense and allows students to see the reasonableness, or unreasonableness, of answers.

The distributive property shows us that numbers can be broken apart in varied ways (e.g., $a(b + c) = (a \times b) + (a \times c)$).

In the expression 4×6, the 6 might be broken into 2 threes, so 4×6 is the same as $4 \times (3 + 3)$, which is the same as 4×3 plus 4×3. Or we could split the 6 into $1 + 5$, so 4×6 is the same as $4 \times (1 + 5)$, which is the same as $(4 \times 1) + (4 \times 5)$, and students are likely to be fluent with the math facts 4×1 and 4×5. Splitting a factor into two simpler factors allows students to find unknown products and strengthens their understanding of numbers.

The order of the factors does not change the product (the commutative property).

The knowledge of this property becomes significant for a whole new reason as students continue their goal to master 0–10 facts. By the time we introduce ×6 facts, students who understand the commutative property will realize that they only have to memorize four of these facts—6×6, 6×7, 6×8, and 6×9—as illustrated in the multiplication chart at the beginning of this chapter. The process of memorizing the ×6 facts is now greatly simplified!

Key questions related to the big ideas for ×6 facts:

When 1 factor doubles will the product double? Why?

What patterns do you notice in the multiples of 6?

What is the connection between ×3 and ×6 facts?

What is the connection between ×2 and ×6 facts?

Does the order of the factors affect the product? Give examples to justify your thinking.

If you do not know a ×6 fact, can you break apart one of the factors to find simpler facts that you do know? How will that help you solve the ×6 fact?

Which ×6 facts do you already know? Why? Which facts do you still need to work on?

Our goal is to continually reinforce the big ideas related to math facts as we help students develop multiplication strategies.

Understanding ×6 Facts

Literature Link: *Snowflake Bentley*

Snowflake Bentley, by Jacqueline Briggs Martin (1998), is the true story of Wilson Bentley, who photographed snowflakes in the late 1800s. His photographs revealed that no 2 snowflakes are alike and that most snow crystals have 6 branches, leading us to interesting classroom explorations of multiples of 6.

Before Reading   Ask students if they have ever seen a picture of a single snowflake. Share some of the pictures from the book. Have students think of words to describe the snowflakes. How are the snowflakes alike and different? Tell students that you will be reading a story about a man who loved the snow. Ask them to listen for facts about snowflakes.

During Reading   As the story is read, emphasize some of the snowflake facts that are shared, particularly those that focus on how snowflakes are alike and how they are different. Some significant facts include:

- Most snowflakes have 6 branches (but a few have 3 branches).

- No snowflake design was ever repeated (no 2 snowflakes look exactly alike).

After Reading   Have students share some facts about snowflakes. Then, pose the following problem:

> Every snowflake is different; however, each snowflake has 6 points. What is the total number of points Willie would count if 7 snowflakes fell on his tray?

Ask students to find a way to solve the problem without counting every point. Have students work on the problem with partners and then share their solutions with the class. Did students need to count every point? Did some skip-count or draw pictures to solve the problem? Skip-counting becomes more difficult as students move beyond the foundation facts, because they are not as familiar with the counting sequences. They may now rely on drawing pictures, repeated addition, or familiar facts to find answers to unknown math facts. On the board, record the multiplication equation shared by students ($7 \times 6 = 42$) and model a drawing of the 7 snowflakes on Willie's tray. (You might simply model a snowflake by creating an X with a line drawn vertically through the middle to represent the 6 branches.)

Have students continue the exploration with the following problem:

> How many points would there be if 1–10 snowflakes fell on Willie's tray? Write multiplication equations to show the number of points for each amount of snowflakes.

Remind students to think about the commutative property. Once they determine the math fact that fits each situation, they may find that they already know the answer from their previous lessons. Have students record their work using the *How Many Points?* recording sheet (see the CD). There is room for students to draw a model to find the answer for facts they do not know (see Figure 9.1).

Once they have completed the task, have students share their multiplication equations with partners. Highlight the products of ×6 facts by recording the multiplication equations on the board. Recording them in order (e.g., 1–10) helps students identify patterns.

Ask students to predict how they think the products would change if the snowflakes had 3 points, like a few snowflakes do. After sharing their

Figure 9.1 *This student's work shows that he has recall of some ×6 facts, but must use drawings to determine the answers to unknown facts.*

How Many Points?

Every snowflake has six points. How many points would Willie have altogether if 1–10 snowflakes fell on his tray.

Number of Snowflakes	Number of Total Points	Multiplication Equation (Draw a model, too, if it helps!)
1	6	6×1
2	12	6×2
3	18	6×3
4	24	6×4
5	30	6×5
6	36	XXXXX X 6×6
7	42	XX XX X X 6×7
8	48	XXXXXX 6×8
9	54	XXXXXXXX 9×6
10	60	10×6

predictions, students work with partners to record equations to show the total number of points there would be if 1–10 3-pointed snowflakes fell on Willie's tray. This provides a nice review of ×3 facts. Have them share their solutions with the class.

After finding solutions for both the 6-pointed and 3-pointed snowflake problems, have students talk with partners to compare the products of ×6 facts and ×3 facts. What do they notice? Allow students to share their ideas and be sure to highlight the important observation, which is sure to come up in your discussions, that the product of a ×6 fact is double the product of a ×3 fact. Have students explain why this is true. Ask students how knowing this connection might help them remember this new set of facts (see Figure 9.2).

Exploring the Facts: Examining Polygons

Exploring attributes of polygons is a great way to connect geometry and multiplication and strengthen students' understanding of both. By exploring the number of sides on sets of hexagons, triangles, and pentagons, students discover connections between math facts.

Hexagons are the perfect polygon for developing multiples of 6. Ask students to work with partners to determine the total number of sides for 6–10 hexagons. Having polygon manipulatives available will provide some students with the visual support they need. Others may draw diagrams or use number strategies to find the products. Have students record multiplication equations to show the total number of sides (i.e., for 6 hexagons, with 6 sides each, students record $6 \times 6 = 36$). Have partners share how they found their answers. Did they draw diagrams? Did they use repeated addition? Did they use the commutative property to solve the ×10 fact? Did they double a known ×3 fact?

Then, begin an exploration to compare the total number of sides on sets of hexagons and triangles. Using the *Multiplication Shapes* recording sheet (see CD), or simply recording in a math journal or on blank paper, ask students to work with partners to determine the total number of sides for the following sets of polygons.

Figure 9.2 *This student describes her observations and tells how they might help her with an unknown ×6 fact.*

What do you notice about the products of 3 and 6?

The products of 3 and 6 are halfs of each other because I saw that 3 was 1/2 of 6 and 30 was 1/2 of 60.

How could knowing the products of 3 help you figure out the products of 6?

Knowing the products of 3 helped me figure out the products of 6 (times 2).

3 hexagons and 3 triangles

5 hexagons and 5 triangles

7 hexagons and 7 triangles

Allow students to use models of the shapes if needed (see Figure 9.3), but ask them to record multiplication and addition equations to show their solutions (i.e., $3 \times 6 = 18$ and $3 \times 3 = 9$; $18 + 9 = 27$ total sides). If some student pairs finish early, simply pose similar problems with different quantities of polygons (e.g., 6 hexagons and 6 triangles). Support student pairs who may be struggling by posing questions to guide their thinking as they explore the task (i.e., How many total sides will there be on the hexagons? How many total sides will there be on the triangles?). Once all students have completed the three sets of data, have them share their answers with the class and then discuss and write about the following.

What do you notice about the total number of sides for hexagons compared to triangles?

Insights will likely include:

The total number of sides for hexagons is always more than the number of sides for the same number of triangles.

The total number of sides for hexagons is double the number of sides for the same number of triangles.

You could just double the number of sides on the triangles to get the sides on the hexagons!

That's right, because a hexagon has twice as many sides! It has 6 sides and a triangle just has 3!

Next, begin an exploration to compare the total number of sides on sets of hexagons and pentagons. Ask students to determine the total number of sides for the following sets.

3 hexagons and 3 pentagons

5 hexagons and 5 pentagons

7 hexagons and 7 pentagons

Figure 9.3 *Students use triangles and hexagons to compare the number of sides for groups of polygons.*

Then, have students share their answers with partners and discuss their observations. Insights will likely include:

The number of sides for the hexagons is always more than the number of sides for pentagons.

If you compare the sides for pentagons and hexagons (or subtract the pentagon sides from hexagon sides) you always get the number of polygons you had (e.g., 3 hexagons have 18 sides and 3 pentagons have 15 sides and 18 – 15 = 3, which is how many hexagons or pentagons we had!).

Look at our number sentences. The difference between the products is the other factor (e.g., 3).

That makes sense because there is always 1 more side on each hexagon. First they had 5 sides, then they each have 6 sides.

Insights about the connection between ×5 and ×6 facts add another layer to students' understandings about numbers.

Supporting All Learners

Following are additional activities for those who need repeated exposure to ×6 facts.

Breaking Apart Factors   Students who understand numbers find multiple ways to get to solutions. Use manipulatives to help students visualize ways to break factors apart to find products.

Use linking cubes to make 4 chains of 6 cubes each. Have students find the product for 4 sets of 6 cubes (e.g., 4 × 6 = 24). Then, break each 6-chain into a chain of 5 cubes and a single cube. Notice that the factor 6 is now broken into 5 + 1, both simpler factors that students have already mastered. Ask students how many cubes there are with 4 chains of 5 cubes (4 × 5 = 20). Ask them how many cubes there are with 4 single cubes (4 × 1 = 4). Ask them how many cubes there are altogether (20 + 4 cubes). How does that compare with their solution to 6 × 4? If they get stuck with ×6 math facts, could they break the 6 apart into 5 and 1? Why would 5 and 1 be good choices (easy numbers to work with)? Are there other ways they might break apart 6 (e.g., 3 + 3 or 4 + 2)? Will this work for other math facts, too? Encourage students to test this idea with other facts. Although our goal is fluency with math facts, students who recognize the flexibility of numbers develop strategies for finding solutions and expand their understanding of multiplication. After modeling the concept, students might use the recording sheet *There's Always Another Way*, found on the CD, to explore this concept.

Exploring Math Facts Using a Ratio Table   Ratio tables provide a great opportunity to practice math facts using real data. Challenge students to brainstorm things that come in sixes (e.g., 6 legs on an insect, 6 sodas in a pack, 6 faces on dice, 6 strings on a guitar). Select a real-world 6, like 6 legs on a cricket, and guide students in solving problems related to your scenario and then recording the products on a ratio table (see Figure 9.4).

> There are 6 legs on every cricket. Complete the table to show how many legs are on the crickets.

It does not matter if the table is horizontal or vertical, but by organizing the data on a table, students notice patterns (i.e., in the legs row, it is adding 6 each time) and functions (i.e., the number of legs is 6 times the number of crickets). Posing problems like "How many legs are on 4 crickets?" or "Jenny

Tip   Narrowing Our Focus with the Commutative Property

Many students become overwhelmed by large sets of facts to memorize. Help relieve their anxiety by giving students a set of ×6 fact cards (see CD). Have them work with partners to sort the cards into two sets: facts we know and facts we still have to learn. Remind them of the commutative property before they begin to sort. Share their excitement when they discover that all they need to learn is 6 × 6, 6 × 7, 6 × 8, 6 × 9!

Figure 9.4 *Ratio tables highlight the patterns in math facts.*

Number of crickets	1	2	3	4	5	6	7	8	9	10
Number of legs	6	12	18	24	30	36	42	48	54	60

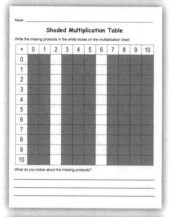

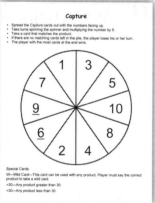

counted 18 legs. How many crickets did she see?" allows students to use the ratio table to locate answers and elevates the math facts practice to a problem-solving experience.

You might complete one table using a guided approach with the class or small group, and then have students work in pairs or independently to complete similar tables with a different 6-legged insect or a different real-world 6 (see template for *Marching Ants* and *Guitar Strings* on the CD).

Comparing Multiples   Have each student complete a shaded multiplication table for ×2 and ×6 facts (see the CD), then pose questions like the following:

> *Do you think there is a connection between ×2 and ×6 facts?*
> *What do you notice about the products?*
> *Can you explain your observations? Do they make sense?*

Students' comments will likely include:

> *The multiples of 6 are always greater than the multiples of 2.*
> *The multiples of 6 are like adding the number 3 times.*
> *The multiples of 6 are triple the multiples of 2.*

Challenge students to test if their conclusions will always be true. Their conclusions relate to some of the big ideas discussed earlier in the chapter and strengthen their understanding of numbers.

Building Automaticity

Targeted Practice

Capture   *Capture* is a fact card game for two or three students. Students spread out the *Capture* cards, showing multiples of 6 (see CD), faceup. Players take turns spinning a number and multiplying by 6. If the product appears on one of the *Capture* cards, the player takes the card. If a product is not there, the player loses his turn. The player who captures the most cards wins the game. *Capture* can also be played with two wild cards that players can use for any product and two cards that can be used to capture products that are greater or less than 30.

Managing Math Games   In order for math game time to go smoothly, students must know the rules for the game and they must know your expectations for their behavior as they play the game. Consider the following questions:

Where can they play the game? At their seat? On the floor? At a designated center?

What is an acceptable voice level?

How many times can they play the game? Is there a time limit? What if they finish the game before the allotted time is over?

Should they hand in their recording sheet? If so, where?

What is their responsibility for cleaning up after they finish the game?

What is the consequence if they do not play appropriately?

It is not important that we all have the same answer for these questions, but it is important that your students know your answers to each question. There are many silent math fact practice tasks that can take the place of math games for a student who is ignoring your procedures. Taking away the privilege of game play for the day is a reasonable consequence. Each student can start fresh again tomorrow, hopefully remembering that ignoring your procedures will result in the natural consequence of practicing alone.

Multiples of 6 Bingo   This version of the familiar game of bingo targets specific math facts and allows students to play, and practice facts, without teacher involvement. Students simply fill a blank 4 × 4 grid (see CD) by recording multiples of 6: 0, 6, 12, 18, 24, 30, 36, 42, 48, 54, 60. Students may record each multiple in any section on their bingo grid, and because there are 16 sections on the grid, students will have to duplicate a few multiples to fill the grid. Let's add an additional 54, 48, 42, 36, and 24 to provide repeated practice with the more difficult ×6 facts! Once players have filled their cards with multiples of 6, play begins. Players can play in pairs or teams of three or four. One player (any player) picks a card from a deck consisting of 0–10 number cards (see card templates on CD). All players multiply the picked number by 6 and cover the product in one place that it appears on their cards. If a player has already covered the product, she cannot cover anything on that turn. Play continues until someone gets bingo (four in a row vertically, horizontally, or diagonally). If all of the 0–10 cards are picked and no player has bingo yet, have students shuffle the cards and continue playing until someone gets bingo. Then players remove the markers from their bingo grids,

shuffle the 0–10 cards, and play again. This game can be modified for any set of math facts.

Tip Remind students to verbalize the math facts as they play games. Saying and hearing math facts supports students' recall of the facts.

Fact Cards to Review Sixes Offering a menu of home ideas for using fact cards can help parents identify effective ways to support their children at home. Identifying and sending home specific fact cards will ensure that students get practice with the needed facts. See the customizable parent letter on the CD, which provides ideas for home practice as well as an explanation for going beyond speed and memory when addressing math facts with their children.

Circles of Dots Provide students with a set of ×6 fact cards and a dot paper recording sheet (see CD). Have students select a fact card (e.g., 6 × 3) and represent the fact by circling 6 rows of 3 dots in each row. Students then find the product, record the multiplication equation, and then select a new fact card and begin again.

Monitoring Progress: Teacher Observation

As students work to master their ×6 facts, frequently move through the room observing partners at work. Which students are automatic in their math fact recall? Which students are relying on strategies to determine the products rather than moving toward automatic recall? Which students are giving incorrect responses or require tools to find products (e.g., multiplication charts, calculators)? Listening to students' verbalizations as they explore math facts activities will provide great insight into their understanding and fluency and will allow you to determine appropriate interventions for strengthening either understanding or automaticity. For ideas on recording observations about automaticity, see the Classroom Observation of Automaticity recording sheet on the Assessment Tools section of the CD.

Tip Fact checks are only one way to assess fluency. Teacher observations and student interviews provide helpful assessment information. See the assessment section of the CD for ideas on conducting automaticity interviews.

Connecting to Division

As students develop an understanding of multiplication with 6 as a factor, take every opportunity to talk about the connection between multiplication and division facts.

You might talk about soft drinks and how they are often sold in packs of 6 bottles. Pose the following problem for students to solve with partners. Provide them with cubes or counters to explore the problem.

> Mrs. Alexander bought some 6-packs of root beer. She had 42 bottles altogether. How many 6-packs did she buy?

Have students share their solutions and ask them about the operation they used to solve it. Some students might share that they divided the total bottles into groups of 6, and others might share that they thought of it as "6 times what equals 42?" Because of the connection between multiplication and division, either of those strategies lead to the answer. Record both equations on the board (e.g., $42 \div 6 = \underline{7}$ or $6 \times \underline{7} = 42$).

Have students continue the exploration by providing them with a ratio table similar to the cricket table they created when exploring multiplication. This time, have the number of individual bottles recorded on the table and ask students to determine and record the number of 6-packs (see Figure 9.5). Discuss the completed ratio table to encourage observations about division.

Modifying *Multiplication Shapes*

The activity *Multiplication Shapes*, mentioned earlier in this chapter, can be modified to develop student understanding of division. To do this, tell students the total number of sides and ask them to determine the number of hexagons. Students can work on the problem with hexagon blocks or by drawing pictures. After doing so, encourage students to write division equations and have them identify what each number in the equation represents.

Figure 9.5 *Ratio tables also provide practice with division facts.*

Number of 6-packs				4			7			
Number of bottles	6	12	18	24	30	36	42	48	54	60

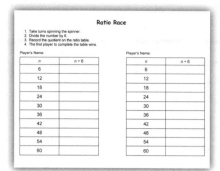

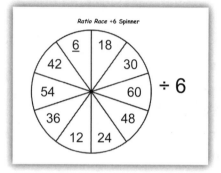

Ratio Race

After students have explored multiplication or division with ratio tables, students can play *Ratio Race*. In this game, players spin numbers and divide by 6. They then write the quotient in the appropriate space in their ratio table. If a quotient is already recorded, the player loses his turn. The first player to complete his ratio table is the winner.

CHAPTER TEN

Multiplying by 9

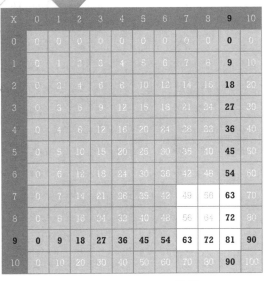

X	0	1	2	3	4	5	6	7	8	9	10
0	0	0	0	0	0	0	0	0	0	0	0
1	0	1	2	3	4	5	6	7	8	9	10
2	0	2	4	6	8	10	12	14	16	18	20
3	0	3	6	9	12	15	18	21	24	27	30
4	0	4	8	12	16	20	24	28	32	36	40
5	0	5	10	15	20	25	30	35	40	45	50
6	0	6	12	18	24	30	36	42	48	54	60
7	0	7	14	21	28	35	42	49	56	63	70
8	0	8	16	24	32	40	48	56	64	72	80
9	0	9	18	27	36	45	54	63	72	81	90
10	0	10	20	30	40	50	60	70	80	90	100

KNOWN FACTS   **9** TARGETED FACTS   UNKNOWN FACTS

After focusing on the ×6 facts, it would be natural to assume that the ×7 facts would be next, but because of our focus on linking unknown facts to known facts, addressing facts with 9 as a factor makes more sense. The ×9 facts are often perceived to be the most difficult, but because of their connection to ×10 facts and their strong reliance on patterns, they are actually much easier to master than students think. Our explorations will focus on observing important patterns when 9 is a factor, as well as using our understanding of ×10 facts to better understand this new set of facts.

Focusing on the Big Ideas

Exploring big ideas about mathematics provides the backdrop for our exploration of 9 as a factor. Following are big ideas for ×9 facts.

Our number system is a system of patterns.

Noticing that the products of ×9 facts create patterns will help students identify pattern-based ways to find ×9 products. Knowing patterns makes the products predictable.

Multiplication facts are connected. Knowing one set of facts can help us understand a related set of facts.

Numbers make sense. They are connected in predictable ways. Products of ×9 facts are 1 group less than products of ×10 facts, so our prior knowledge of multiples of 10 can help us quickly learn to multiply by 9 (i.e., 9×3 equals 1 group of 3 less than 10×3 or might be thought of as $30 - 3$). This big idea brings understanding to math facts and helps in the development of number sense.

The order of the factors does not affect the product.

Again, an understanding of the commutative property simplifies the task of mastering math facts. By the time we introduce ×9 facts, students who understand the commutative property realize that they only have 3 facts to memorize: 9×7, 9×8, and 9×9.

Key questions related to the big ideas for ×9 facts:

How are ×9 facts related to ×10 facts?

What patterns do you notice in the multiples of 9?

When multiplying by 9, do you immediately know the tens digit of the product? Why?

Which ×9 facts do you already know? Why? Which facts will you still need to memorize?

Tip Often thought of as the most difficult math facts, a focus on patterns will show students the simplicity of the ×9 facts.

Our goal is to continually reinforce the big ideas related to math facts as we help students develop multiplication strategies.

Understanding ×9 Facts

Literature Link: *Cloudy with a Chance of Meatballs*

In *Cloudy with a Chance of Meatballs*, Judi Barrett (1978) tells the story of the unusual weather in the town of Chewandswallow, where food and drink fall from the sky. The story serves up an opportunity for multiplying by 9 in an intriguing context.

Before Reading   Before beginning the story, show the students the cover illustration and read the title. Ask them to turn to a partner to predict what the story will be about. After sharing some predictions, ask students to imagine what it might be like if it rained meatballs. What other foods might fall from the sky where the man on the cover lives?

During Reading   Ask students to listen to the story to hear about some very unusual weather in a very unusual town.

After Reading   Give students paper plates and explain that as citizens of Chewandswallow they will have to go outside to catch meatballs on their paper plates for dinner, just like the citizens of the town did. Assign partners. Have one partner draw 9 meatballs on his paper plate and the other partner draw 10 meatballs on her paper plate. Ask partners to decide how many total meatballs would be collected if 7 people each caught 9 meatballs? Provide students with paper to draw a model and write an equation to show their solution. Ask partners to figure out how many total meatballs would be collected if 7 people each caught 10 meatballs. Again, have them draw a model and write an equation to show their solution.

To check students' work, invite 7 students to stand in the front of the room with their paper plates showing 9 meatballs each. After the total is found and recorded for 7 plates of 9 meatballs, the same can be done with 7 plates of 10 meatballs. Have partners check their solutions and then compare the products and discuss their insights. After students share their thoughts, be sure to highlight the observation that 63 (the total for 9 meatballs on each plate) is *7 less than 70* (the total for 10 meatballs on each plate). Is that a coincidence? Ask partners to predict if they think this will always be true. Anytime they multiply a number by 9, will it be that number less than multiplying it by 10? Why might that be true?

Have partners test their predictions by discussing the total number of meatballs collected by 8 students collecting 9 meatballs compared with 8 students collecting 10 meatballs. After students draw a model and write a multiplication equation for each, have students share their findings. Invite 8 students to stand in the front of the room with their paper plates showing 9 meatballs each. After the total is found and recorded for 8 plates of 9 meatballs, the same can be done with 8 plates of 10 meatballs. Again, have students compare and discuss the results. Are 8 groups of 9 meatballs 8 less than 8 groups of 10 meatballs?

Have students work with partners to continue investigating the connection between ×9 and ×10 products. Have them create a list of ×9 facts with factors of 1–8 and a list of ×10 facts with factors of 1–8, or they might use the *Plates of Meatballs* template on the CD to record their data (see Figure 10.1). Challenge students to explain the connection between the ×9 and ×10 products.

Finally, ask students to predict the total number of meatballs for 9 plates with 9 meatballs on each plate. Challenge them to use what they have observed about ×10 products to help them figure out the answer. Have students share how they arrived at their answers (i.e., "9 plates with 10 meatballs on each plate is 90 meatballs, so it would be 9 less than 90. It would be 81 meatballs.").

Exploring the Facts: Observing Patterns

Have students record the products for ×9 facts from 1 to 10 (see the *Observing Nines* recording sheet on the CD). Once students have completed the facts, have them work with partners to check their answers or review the answers together. If necessary, allow them to use a multiplication chart to locate the products. For this activity, which involves observing patterns in the multiples of 9, it is important that all students are observing correct products.

Once products are verified, ask students to work with partners to examine the math facts, looking for any patterns they might see, and to record their observations (see Figure 10.2). Once students have recorded observations, guide them in a discussion to focus on the patterns they have noticed. Observations will likely include:

- The multiples of 9 are 9, 18, 27, 36 … which is counting by nines or adding 9 more each time.
- The digits in the multiples of 9 all add up to 9 (i.e., in 18, $1 + 8 = 9$; in 27, $2 + 7 = 9$).

- The digits are reversed for some multiples of 9 (e.g., 45 and 54; 36 and 63; 27 and 72).

- As the tens digits increase by one ten, the ones digits decrease by 1 (e.g., 09, 18, 27, 36 …).

- The tens digit of the product is always 1 less than the factor being multiplied by 9 (e.g., 9 × 8 is 72 and 7 is 1 less than the factor 8; 9 × 5 is 45 and 4 is 1 less than the factor 5).

Figure 10.1 *This student uses his understanding of the connection between ×9 and ×10 facts to make an accurate prediction.*

Plates of Meatballs

Complete the tables below to show how many meatballs were collected by people who caught 9 on their plate and those who caught 10 on their plate.

Number of People	Number of Meatballs on Each Plate	Total Number of Meatballs	Number of People	Number of Meatballs on Each Plate	Total Number of Meatballs
1	× 9 =	9	1	× 10 =	10
2	× 9 =	18	2	× 10 =	20
3	× 9 =	27	3	× 10 =	30
4	× 9 =	36	4	× 10 =	40
5	× 9	45	5	× 10 =	50
6	× 9	54	6	× 10 =	60
7	× 9	63	7	× 10 =	70
8	× 9	72	8	× 10	80

What do you notice about the connection between the ×9 and ×10 facts?

It's just 1 number less 2×9 is ② less than than 2×10 or 3×9 is ③ less than 30

Predict the total number of meatballs for nine plates with nine meatballs on each plate. __81__

Would knowing how many meatballs were on nine plates with ten meatballs on each plate help you with your prediction? How?

Yes because I could just 9×10 and 1 less is 81

Figure 10.2 *Asking students to record their observations focuses them on finding patterns in math facts.*

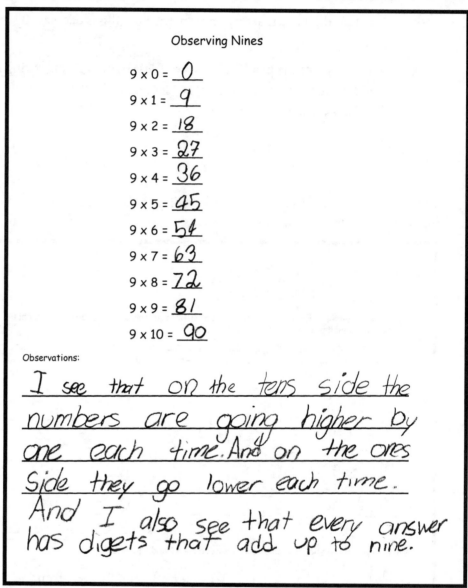

Observing Nines

9 x 0 = _0_

9 x 1 = _9_

9 x 2 = _18_

9 x 3 = _27_

9 x 4 = _36_

9 x 5 = _45_

9 x 6 = _54_

9 x 7 = _63_

9 x 8 = _72_

9 x 9 = _81_

9 x 10 = _90_

Observations:

I see that on the tens side the numbers are going higher by one each time. And on the ones side they go lower each time. And I also see that every answer has digets that add up to nine.

Some questions to stimulate thinking:

If you forget a ×9 fact, will you always know how the product begins (tens digit)? Why?

If you know the tens digit, can you figure out the ones digit? How?

Although understanding the connection between ×9 facts and ×10 facts builds understanding of number concepts, the observation of patterns greatly supports fluency. Have students try a few ×9 facts for fluency, reminding them to begin the product with a tens digit that is 1 less than the factor (e.g., 9 ×

7 = 6_). Simple knowledge of digits that add to 9 will give them the rest of the product (e.g., 6 + 3 = 9, so 63 is the product). Keep in mind, students have studied all but three of the ×9 facts (9 × 7, 9 × 8, 9 × 9), so repeated focus on those facts will help students gain automaticity.

Supporting All Learners

The following ×9 fact activities will support students who need additional exposure to the concept.

Exploring Common Errors   Earlier, when discussing the advantages of observing patterns in ×9 facts, we emphasized the idea that the tens digit of the product is always 1 less than the factor. This insight will eliminate common errors that occur as students confuse the products of 9 × 5 and 9 × 6. Because the products have the same digits, 45 and 54, they are easily confused unless students think about reasonableness. If the factor is 5, the product will have a 4 as the tens digit. 54 would not make sense for 9 × 5 because 10 × 5 is 50 and 9 × 5 is less than 10 × 5.

Provide students with some ×9 fact statements and ask them to decide if they are correct or not, and to justify their decisions.

$$9 \times 6 = 45 \qquad\qquad 9 \times 7 = 63$$
$$9 \times 9 = 72 \qquad\qquad 9 \times 3 = 18$$

Can your students verbalize why the incorrect statements do not make sense? Have they developed the understanding that allows them to spot errors?

Exploring ×9 Facts Through Ten-Chains   Have students create a specific amount of ten-chains (e.g., 6) with linking cubes. Have students skip-count to find the total number of cubes in their 6 chains of 10. Ask students to remove 1 cube from each chain and find the new total of 6 chains of 9. Ask questions to guide students in developing the connection between ×9 and ×10 facts.

> *How many cubes were removed (6)?*
> *What is the difference between the ×10 product and the ×9 product (6)?*
> *Does that make sense? Why or why not?*

Have students repeat the investigation with other quantities of ten-chains and nine-chains. This activity helps students visualize the difference between multiplying by 9 and 10.

Tip   **Hand Tricks**

Although there are lots of hand tricks that are fun to experience and that allow students to find multiples of 9, remember that our goals are understanding and automaticity. Hand tricks do not develop number sense (as in exploring connections to 10 or observing patterns) and do not support fluency. Try to focus on a technique that explores numbers rather than simply showing solutions.

Tip **Narrowing Our Focus with the Commutative Property**

Many students become overwhelmed by large sets of facts to memorize. Help relieve their anxiety by giving students a set of ×9 fact cards. Have students work with partners to sort the cards into two sets: facts we know and facts we still have to learn. Remind them of the commutative property before they begin to sort. Share their excitement when they discover that all they need to learn is 9 × 7, 9 × 8, and 9 × 9! Remind them of the "trick" for ×9 facts (i.e., for 9 × 7, the tens digit is 6 and 6 + 3 = 9, so the product is 63).

Writing to Explain   It is helpful to know what students are thinking as they process each new set of facts. In addition to oral explanations, it can be helpful for students to write about their thinking (see Figure 10.3). Try this prompt:

> A friend is having a difficult time remembering ×9 multiplication facts. What would you tell him to help him with these facts?

Take every opportunity to prompt students to write about their mathematical thinking. The insights will allow you to design instruction and tailor interventions to meet their needs.

Predict and Check with a Calculator   Students working to master their basic facts can utilize a calculator in various ways. Students might use calculators as an accuracy tool when working independently or playing math fact games with classmates. Calculators can also be integrated into facts practice tasks like *Predict and Check* (see CD template) in which students begin by predicting the products of a list of math facts. After predicting the product of each fact, students compare their predictions to those of their partner or check their work with a calculator. Students should be encouraged to note the facts that they correctly predicted and the facts that they need to work on.

Name: _____

Predict and Check ×9 Facts

Predict the product of each fact. After writing all of your predictions, check your predictions with a calculator.

Predictions	Calculator Check
0 × 9 =	0 × 9 =
10 × 9 =	10 × 9 =
9 × 2 =	9 × 2 =
9 × 8 =	9 × 8 =
3 × 9 =	3 × 9 =
5 × 9 =	5 × 9 =
9 × 7 =	9 × 7 =
9 × 9 =	9 × 9 =
9 × 6 =	9 × 6 =
9 × 4 =	9 × 4 =

Write the facts that you correctly predicted.

_____
_____
_____
_____
_____

Write the facts you need to practice.

_____
_____
_____
_____
_____

Figure 10.3 *This student shares his insights about ×9 facts.*

What advice would you give a friend who is having a hard time learning x9 facts?

The number you multiplicy nine by is how many less than if you multiplicy it by 10. Plus the digits in the product add up to nine. And I would tell them to Practice.

Building Automaticity

Targeted Practice

After students have engaged in a variety of activities to understand multiplication with 9 as a factor, it is time to provide them with repeated opportunities to practice the facts.

> **Talking About Facts** Many students retain facts more readily if they verbalize the facts. Rather than simply looking at facts and "doing them in their head," encourage students to verbalize as they play math games. Each time students repeat the math fact, they are working on committing that fact to memory. In addition, when math facts are verbalized, partners are more likely to catch each other's errors. And in math games, it is important that partners know what each other is thinking. Silent games, in which students simply place a marker on a number, can leave one partner wondering what the other has done. Encourage students to talk as they think about math facts.

Condition *Condition* is a game that offers practice with place value and comparing numbers while developing automaticity with ×9 facts. Students spread *Condition* cards out on the desk, facedown. The *Condition* cards have statements, or conditions, such as "Product is greater than 40" or "Product has a 3 in it." The number cards are shuffled and placed facedown in a stack. A player turns over the top number card and multiplies by 9. He then turns over a *Condition* card. If the product meets the condition of the turned-over card, the player keeps the *Condition* card. If the product does not meet the condition, it is his opponent's turn. The player with the most *Condition* cards at the end of the game wins.

Nine Cross In this game, students work to fill a row or column on the *Nine Cross* game board (see CD). Each partner has her own game board, and partners share a deck of cards that consists of two sets of 0–10 cards shuffled together and placed facedown (see card templates on CD). Partners take turns selecting a card from the deck, multiplying by 9, and recording the product on their *Nine Cross* game board. The first player to complete a row or column wins. Feel free to vary the game so students must complete the entire cross in order to win.

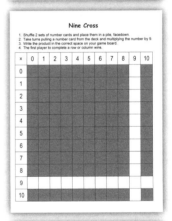

Optimizing Fact Card Reviews   As we explored the teaching of math facts, we began to rethink some traditional classroom games played with fact cards. To alleviate anxiety and ensure that the students who need the fact practice stay engaged in the activities, we recommend fact card activities that do not eliminate the students who struggle with facts because they need the practice most. In addition, speed competitions (e.g., one student pitted against another) generally end in frustration for the students who need the practice provided by the game. Fact card activities that ensure continued involvement of all students best meet our instructional goals.

Highs and Lows   *Highs and Lows* can be played with a partner or alone. The ×9 fact cards are shuffled and laid out in a row facedown. The first card is flipped over and the player tells the product. Before flipping over the next card, the player predicts whether the product will be higher or lower than the previous card. If correct, the player continues on to the next facedown card, predicting whether the product will be higher or lower than the card before it. The goal of the game is to successfully predict all of the cards. If a player's prediction is incorrect, all of the cards are picked up, shuffled, and the game starts over.

Monitoring Progress: Writing About Learning Math Facts

Students can share their understanding of math facts through writing. Journal prompts might include:

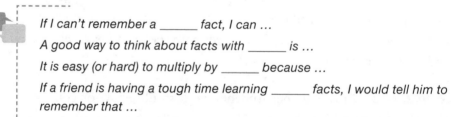

If I can't remember a _____ fact, I can …

A good way to think about facts with _____ is …

It is easy (or hard) to multiply by _____ because …

If a friend is having a tough time learning _____ facts, I would tell him to remember that …

Following a fact check, students might write a plan for addressing unknown facts (see Figure 10.4).

Tip   **Modifying Activities from Previous Chapters**

Remember that activities from previous chapters can be easily adapted for ×9 facts. You might want to try:

Fact Sorting (Chapter Six)

Circles of Dots (Chapter Nine)

Multiples Bingo (Chapter Nine)

Figure 10.4 *During the teacher-student conference following a fact check, strengths and needs are identified. Following the conference, this student will write about her strengths and her plan for mastery of the unknown facts.*

Connecting to Division

Pull out those triangle fact cards! Triangle fact cards (see CD templates) reinforce the connection between multiplication and division facts and help students work toward mastery of both. The three angles of the triangle hold the two factors and the product (or the dividend, divisor, and quotient if we are speaking about division). See Chapter Seven for an introduction to triangle fact cards.

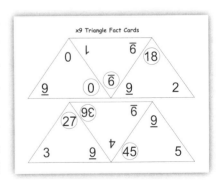

Have partners select a triangle fact card and write two multiplication and two division equations for the card. This fact family practice reminds students of the link between multiplication and division. And remind students that when it comes to fluency, *think multiplication.* 63 ÷ 9 might be thought of as "What times 9 equals 63?"

Ps and Qs (Products and Quotients)

It is common practice to reference multiplication facts when trying to remember a quotient. *Ps and Qs* is a fact card game that helps students connect division facts with multiplication facts. Students spread out a set of multiplication and division fact cards facedown. Players take turns flipping cards over to make a match, similar to traditional matching games like *Memory* or *Concentration*. The difference in this game is that a player must state the product or quotient for the first card he flips over. If correct, the player may try to make a match. If incorrect, the player loses his turn. Matches in this game are made of one multiplication fact connected to a related division fact (e.g., 7 × 9 matches 63 ÷ 9 or 63 ÷ 7).

CHAPTER ELEVEN

Multiplying by 8

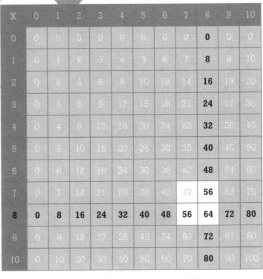

Our students have now explored nearly all of their math facts, although they are still working on their automaticity with the facts. We will explore the ×8 facts next, building on students' understanding of doubling and their previous work with ×2 and ×4 facts. You may notice that the Multiplying by 8 and Multiplying by 7 chapters are a bit shorter than the previous chapters. At this point, our students have had many experiences with the concept of multiplication and it is much easier for them to plug in new sets of facts to their previous understandings. And

KNOWN FACTS | 8 TARGETED FACTS | UNKNOWN FACTS

141

although students have not yet been introduced to the ×8 facts, the only ×8 facts that are new to them are 8 × 7 and 8 × 8.

Focusing on the Big Ideas

Exploring big ideas about mathematics provides the backdrop for our exploration of 8 as a factor. Following are big ideas for ×8 facts.

Multiplication by 8 is double multiplication by 4.

Students have already explored doubling when they investigated ×2 facts. Multiplying by 4 was seen as simply doubling the product of the ×2 fact. And multiplying by 8 is doubling the product of the ×4 fact. Multiplying by 8 might be thought of as doubling, doubling, and doubling again.

Our number system is a system of patterns.

Like all sets of math facts, the ×8 facts create patterns. Noticing that multiples of 8 are always even numbers or realizing that multiples of 8 are also multiples of 4 (and multiples of 2) leads to interesting conversation and insights.

The order of the factors does not affect the product (the commutative property).

Based on this understanding, students realize that they already know most of the ×8 facts. Only 8 × 7 and 8 × 8 are new to them.

Key questions related to the big ideas for ×8 facts:

What patterns do you notice in the products?

What is the relationship between multiples of 4 and multiples of 8?

Are multiples of 8 always multiples of 4? Why?

What is the relationship between multiples of 2 and multiples of 8?

Are all multiples of 8 also multiples of 2? Why?

What does it mean to double, then double, then double again?

Are multiples of 8 always even numbers? Why?

Tip Understanding math properties, like the commutative or distributive properties, builds students understanding of numbers and supports their understanding of math facts.

Our goal is to continually reinforce the big ideas related to math facts as we help students develop multiplication strategies.

Understanding ×8 Facts

Literature Link: *Snowmen at Night*

What do snowmen do when no one is watching? *Snowmen at Night* by Caralyn Buehner (2002) illustrates the adventures snowmen have when everyone else is sleeping. The story provides an engaging context for snowman explorations that highlight the relationships between ×2, ×4, and ×8 facts.

Before Reading   Talk with students about making snowmen. Have they ever made a snowman? What items might they need? Could they make eyes with pinecones? Could they use twigs to make arms? Have students design their own snowmen and use numbers to describe them (i.e., a student might label her snowman with 2 buttons for eyes, 1 scarf, 1 carrot for a nose, and 2 sticks for arms). Students can then share their snowmen with partners.

During Reading   When reading the story, pause occasionally to quickly show students an illustration and have them estimate how many snowmen they think are in that illustration. Have them briefly share how they arrived at their estimations.

After Reading   Draw a snowman on the board, overhead, or chart paper. Be sure that your snowman has 2 pine cones for eyes, 4 rocks for buttons, and 8 pieces of coal for a mouth. Mention that 1 snowman just isn't enough to have fun adventures at night. Instead, you want to build a few more … maybe as many as 10. Divide students into 9 groups and have each group pick a card from a 2–10 deck. Pose the problem below for students to explore with their team (see *Making Snowmen* recording sheet on CD).

> Your number tells how many snowmen we should make. Draw a picture of the snowmen and write three multiplication equations to show how many pinecones, rocks, and pieces of coal we need in order to make that many snowmen.

Move around the room to check that students are talking together about the solution, but ask each student to draw the snowmen and record the equations.

After students have determined how many of each item are needed to build their snowmen, summarize and record the class findings. Begin the class chart with data about the 1 snowman that was done together, then have each group share their findings until you have data for 1–10 snowmen on the chart. Students can record the data on their own charts (see *A Closer Look at*

Snowmen Facts on CD) as in Figure 11.1. After the chart is completed, have partners look for patterns. Students notice:

The number of pieces of coal is always double the number of rocks (the ×8 facts are double the ×4 facts).

The number of rocks is always double the number of pinecones (the ×4 facts are double the ×2 facts).

The number of pieces of coal are always 4 times the number of pinecones (the ×8 facts are 4 times the ×2 facts).

Ask students what they noticed about doubling. Does anyone mention that you can double, double, and double again to find the product of a number and 8? Verbalize this idea if students do not notice it. Ask students if they

Figure 11.1 *Seeing the data recorded on the chart allows students to draw conclusions about the relationships between ×2, ×4, and ×8 facts.*

2 pinecones	4 rocks	8 pieces of coal
1 x 2 = 2	1 x 4 = 4	1 x 8 = 8
2 x 2 = 4	2 x 4 = 8	2 x 8 = 16
3 x 2 = 6	3 x 4 = 12	3 x 8 = 24
4 x 2 = 8	4 x 4 = 16	4 x 8 = 36
5 x 2 = 10	5 x 4 = 20	5 x 8 = 40
6 x 2 = 12	6 x 4 = 24	6 x 8 = 48
7 x 2 = 14	7 x 4 = 28	7 x 8 = 56
8 x 2 = 16	8 x 4 = 32	8 x 8 = 64
9 x 2 = 18	9 x 4 = 36	9 x 8 = 72
10 x 2 = 20	10 x 4 = 40	10 x 8 = 80

How are the products of 2, 4, and 8 related?

They are all doubles double 2 is 4 and double 4 is 8. Plus they are all even.

How could this help you remember the products of 8?

If you know 3x2 you double it to get 12 and double it again to get 3x8=24.

think that this will always be true. Have students work with partners to double, double, double numbers and then use a calculator to check to see if their result is that number ×8. Have the students discuss their findings.

Exploring the Facts: Visualizing Doubles

Explore the double, double, double concept through a hands-on exploration. Provide students with a set of counters. Ask them to select 1 counter. Ask them to double it. How many do they have now (2)? Ask them to double again. How many do they have (4)? Ask them to double again. How many do they have (8)? Have them fold a paper into four columns and record their results as in Figure 11.2. Have students use their counters and explore the double, double, double with other numbers. What do they notice? How would they describe what is happening using multiplication equations? Does it make sense?

Supporting All Learners

The following classroom activities provide you with additional lesson ideas for the whole class or for small teacher-led groups who need to explore ×8 facts in a different way.

Exploring Doubles with Centimeter Grids   Provide students with centimeter grid paper (see CD) and scissors. Have students outline and then cut

Figure 11.2 *This student folded a paper into four columns and recorded her doubling data.*

a number	double it	double it again	double it again
1	2	4	8
2	4	8	16
3	6	12	24
4	8	16	32
5	10	20	40
6	12	24	48
7	14	28	56
8	16	32	64
9	18	36	72
10	20	40	80
	×2	×4	×8

out a 2 × 8 area, labeling it with the math fact, including the product. What would be double that area? 4 × 8? Have them outline and cut out a 4 × 8 area, labeled with the math fact. What would be double that area? 8 × 8? Have them outline and cut out an 8 × 8 area, labeled with the math fact. Do they see the doubles? Students can lay the 2 × 8 on the 4 × 8 to see the double or lay the models side-by-side to view the doubles as in Figure 11.3.

This activity would make an informative bulletin board. Assign varied numbers to students and have them create ×2, ×4, and ×8 area models, labeling each model with the corresponding multiplication fact. Student writing, sharing what they notice about the products, could be included.

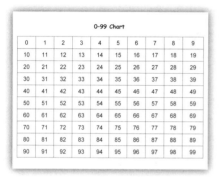

Coloring 0–99 Charts   Provide students with a 0–99 chart (see CD) and have them use a yellow crayon to color all of the multiples of a designated number. Students will quickly see the pattern created by the math fact set and will be able to extend the pattern beyond the basic facts.

Focusing on Targeted Facts   For students who are anxious about the difficulty of ×8 facts, don't forget the sorting activity from Chapter Ten. Give students a set of ×8 fact cards and have them work with partners to sort the

Figure 11.3 *Comparing physical models allows students to see the doubling concept.*

cards into two sets: *facts we have seen* and *new facts*. Remind them of the commutative property before they begin to sort so they recognize that any math fact with a factor that is 0, 1, 2, 3, 4, 5, 6, 9, or 10 is a math fact they have seen before. After their sorting, have them report which facts are new: 8 × 7 and 8 × 8. Give students some index cards and have them record each new fact on a card. If there are any other ×8 facts that they have not yet mastered, allow them to make fact cards for those ×8 facts, too. Encourage them to bring the cards home to practice their facts.

Building Automaticity

Repeated practice will help students commit these ×8 facts to memory. Although there are only two new facts (8 × 7 and 8 × 8), students are likely to still need practice with other ×8 facts to develop automaticity.

Targeted Practice

Ongoing Practice Automaticity with math facts requires practice. Practice should take place on a daily basis while students are learning their facts. And we know that in order to retain their facts, ongoing review will be necessary. Even after students have mastered the facts, provide brief practice several times each week to ensure that students maintain fluency.

Practice can take place during math class or at other times during the school day (i.e., teachers might make games available as students arrive to school in the morning). Many teachers insert quick fact reviews into their lessons on a regular basis. Even a five-minute activity provides repeated exposure to the targeted skills and promotes fluency. Some teachers schedule opportunities several times a week (i.e., ten minutes on Monday, Wednesday, and Friday) for students to engage in paired practice activities, and the teacher works with students who need additional support with their math facts. Even indoor recess provides an opportunity for students to play interactive math fact games. Practice can happen at home, too. Students can use a fact log (see CD) to record when they practice, how long they practice, and the targeted facts. Ongoing opportunities for students to practice math facts through interactive activities and games promote math fact fluency.

Tip **Practicing Targeted Facts**

Students may not need to practice all of the facts in a fact set. Modify games and activities to target specific facts to meet your students' needs.

Missing Numbers   *Missing Numbers* (see CD) is a digit card game in which 0–9 cards are shuffled and placed in a stack facedown. Players take turns flipping a card over and writing the digit in one of the blanks on the *Missing Numbers* game board (i.e., Ronny pulls a 3 so he can complete the multiplication equation $8 \times 4 = \_2$). If a digit can't be used, the card is returned to the deck and the player loses his turn. The first player to complete all of his multiplication equations wins. The game can also be played with two wild cards that can be used for any digit.

Crazy Eight   In this game, students work to cover the large 8 on their game board (see CD template) as they review ×8 facts. Each student has a game board, and a deck of cards, consisting of two sets of 0–10 cards (see CD), is shuffled and placed facedown. Students take turns picking a card, multiplying by 8, and covering the product on their game boards. If a product is already covered, the students must pass for that turn. The first player to cover the whole board is the winner.

Sum Up the Facts   To play *Sum Up the Facts*, students shuffle the ×8 fact cards and take turns with a partner selecting a card from the facedown deck. Each player finds the product, records it, and after 4 rounds, finds the sum of their 4 products. The player with the largest sum (or smallest, if you'd prefer) wins.

Monitoring Progress: Dealing with Anxiety

Observe students for signs of anxiety during Fact Checks. Are there students who get anxious as soon as a Fact Check is mentioned? High anxiety might indicate the need to modify the Fact Check by decreasing the number of facts or allowing the student additional time to complete the task. Once the student experiences success, more facts can be added or the time can be decreased.

Tip   Modifying Activities from Previous Chapters

Remember that games and fact card activities from previous chapters can be easily adapted for ×8 facts. You might want to try:

Multi-Models (Chapter Eight)

Multiples Bingo (Chapter Nine)

Highs and Lows (Chapter Ten)

Player's Name: _____

Missing Numbers

- Shuffle digit cards and place them in a stack.
- Take turns flipping over a digit card.
- Record the digit on one of the lines to complete a multiplication fact.
- After completing the fact, read the fact to your opponent then return the card to the deck.
- If the digit card can't be used you lose your turn.
- The first player to complete every equation wins.

1 × __ = 8	__ × 8 = 8
8 × 2 = __6	__ × 2 = 16
__ × 3 = 24	3 × 8 = __4
8 × __ = 32	4 × 8 = __2
8 × __ = 40	__ × 8 = 40
__ × 6 = 48	6 × __ = 48
8 × 7 = 5__	__ × 7 = 56
8 × 8 = 6__	__ × 8 = 64
8 × __ = 72	9 × 8 = __2
8 × __0 = 80	10 × 8 = 8__

Missing Numbers **Digit Cards**

0	1	2
3	4	5
6	7	8
9	**WILD** Use any digit.	**WILD** Use any digit.

Crazy Eight

- Shuffle the cards and place them in a pile, facedown.
- Take turns picking a card and multiplying by 8.
- Cover the product on your game board.
- If the product is already covered, you lose that turn.
- The first player to cover the whole board is the winner.

72, 64, 48, 16, 80, 8, 0, 40, 32, 24, 56

Crazy Eight **Number Cards**

0	1	2
3	4	5
6	7	8
9	10	

Connecting to Division

Exploring Division Through Real-World Problems

Challenge your students to some spider division. Tell them you will be thinking of a number of spiders, but you will only tell them the total number of legs on the spiders. It will be their job to figure out how many spiders you are thinking of. Begin by saying there are 8 legs. This will let you know whether students know that all spiders have 8 legs, unlike insects that have 6 legs. Be sure to discuss the number of legs on a spider if you notice any confusion. Try some other quantities of legs (e.g., 64, 32, 40, 56 …). Allow students to use paper and pencil if they need to draw diagrams, but emphasize the connection to multiplication. If all spiders have 8 legs, 8 times what number equals 64? Record the division equations on the board as you pose various problems. Then, challenge students to practice with partners using octopus division!

Spaces

Spaces is a game to practice dividing by 8. It can be played by two to four players. The game board is 72 squares, labeled with numbers 1–10. Players put their markers on the start square and take turns spinning numbers and dividing by 8. If the quotient appears on one of the adjacent squares, the player can choose to move his marker to that square. The player loses his turn if the quotient doesn't appear on an adjacent square (e.g., squares that are above, below, right, left, or diagonal to the player's square). The first player to the shaded 8 square wins.

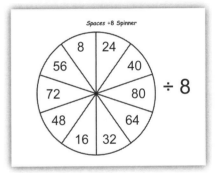

Spaces

All players begin with their chips on START. Spin the spinner to find a quotient. If the quotient is on a space that is above, below, next to, or diagonal to yours, you may move to it. If not, you lose your turn. Take turns spinning and moving toward the shaded 8 space, which is the FINISH. To land on the finish space, you must spin a division fact with the quotient of 8. The first player to land on the finish space wins.

START	3	6	2	3	6	2	1
1	2	8	2	10	3	9	10
4	5	4	3	7	4	10	3
2	1	7	6	1	2	4	10
6	5	1	9	4	9	5	6
7	3	8	2	9	3	10	9
4	5	10	3	4	6	2	5
8	4	1	8	5	2	9	7
3	7	9	2	10	9	5	8

Spaces ÷8 Spinner

8 24 56 40 72 80 48 64 16 32 ÷ 8

Multiplying by 7

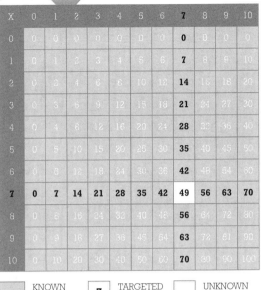

Multiplication with 7 as a factor can be a bit more complex for students to master. The skip-counting patterns are there, but are not very familiar to students. There are no doubles to rely on. The facts are farther from fives and tens, so it is a bit more complex to use those familiar facts to find ×7 products. But our good news is that by studying the facts in this order, there is only one ×7 fact that is new to our students: 7 × 7. When the ×7 facts are introduced last in the sequence, our students are able to rely on all of their other strategies for these facts, because all, except 7 × 7, have been studied as a part of another set of facts.

KNOWN FACTS   **7** TARGETED FACTS   UNKNOWN FACTS

Focusing on the Big Ideas

As we look back on the other factors already studied, we see a variety of strategies that support our students in mastering ×7 facts. When multiplying 7 × 2, students think doubles. When multiplying 7 × 4 or 7 × 8, their doubles understanding is again helpful. Their understanding of the identity property, allows them to understand 7 × 1, and certainly the commutative property assures them that all of the products they have already learned will be the same when the factors are reversed. In addition, the distributive property and the concept of square numbers will support mastery of these facts.

The distributive property shows us that numbers can be broken apart in varied ways (e.g., $a(b + c) = (a \times b) + (a \times c)$).

In the expression 6 × 7, 7 might be broken into 2 + 5, so 6 × 7 is the same as 6 × (2 + 5), which is the same as 6 × 2 plus 6 × 5. Splitting large factors and then finding the sum of the two familiar products is a way to find unknown products.

Multiplying a factor by itself results in a square number.

Students have worked with arrays throughout their study of multiplication. When the factors are the same, the arrays form a square. 7 × 7 is the only math fact that has yet to be addressed. A focus on square numbers allows students to explore this special kind of math fact.

Key questions related to the big ideas for ×7 facts:

> *Does the order of the factors affect the product? Give examples to justify your thinking.*
>
> *Which ×7 facts do you already know? Which facts will you still need to memorize?*
>
> *If you do not know a ×7 fact, can you break apart one of the factors to find simpler facts that you do know? Will that help you find the ×7 fact?*
>
> *What are square numbers? How could you prove that a number is a square number?*

Tip With an understanding of the commutative property, students realize that 7 × 7 is the only ×7 fact they still need to master.

Our goal is to continually reinforce the big ideas related to math facts as we help students develop multiplication strategies.

Understanding ×7 Facts

Literature Link: *Thunder Cake*

Thunder Cake, by Patricia Polacco (1990), tells the story of a grandmother who helps her granddaughter overcome her fear of thunderstorms by baking a thunder cake. As the thunder roars, the duo work together to gather the ingredients for the cake. After gathering eggs, milk, and other ingredients, they bake the cake, frost it with chocolate icing, and then add a final touch of strawberries on top! Seven strawberries! What a delicious way to explore ×7 facts!

Before Reading　Talk with students about thunderstorms. Do they know anyone who is afraid of thunder? Why do they suppose people are afraid of thunder? Tell students that you will be reading a story about a little girl who is afraid of thunder. Ask them to listen to see how she overcomes her fear.

During Reading　Grandma said that if you begin counting when you see lightning and keep counting until you hear the thunder, the number will tell you how many miles away the storm is. Throughout the book, the granddaughter counts to see how close the storm is getting. Have students join in as the little girl counts in a very predictable pattern.

After Reading　Ask students what ingredients are needed to bake thunder cake. Share the thunder cake recipe from the back of the book. Remind students that recipes tell you which ingredients to use and how much of each ingredient. Mention that it does not say how many strawberries to use. Turn to the page with Grandma placing the last strawberry on the cake and count the strawberries with the students. Seven strawberries decorate the cake. Pose the problem below for students to explore with partners (see the *Thunder Cake* activity on the CD).

> **How many strawberries would Grandma need to decorate 7 thunder cakes?**

Remind students that they can solve the problem in a way that works for them. Have manipulatives available for those who request them. After students have had time to explore the problem, have partners share their solutions and strategies with the class. Did students add to find the total number of strawberries? Did they draw pictures as in Figure 12.1? Did they build arrays? Did they use multiplication? If they used multiplication, how did they find the product? Did they begin with a math fact they knew? Did they break apart one of the factors? Write the multiplication equation, $7 \times 7 = 49$, on the board.

Figure 12.1 *Drawing thunder cakes helps this student find the product of 7 × 7.*

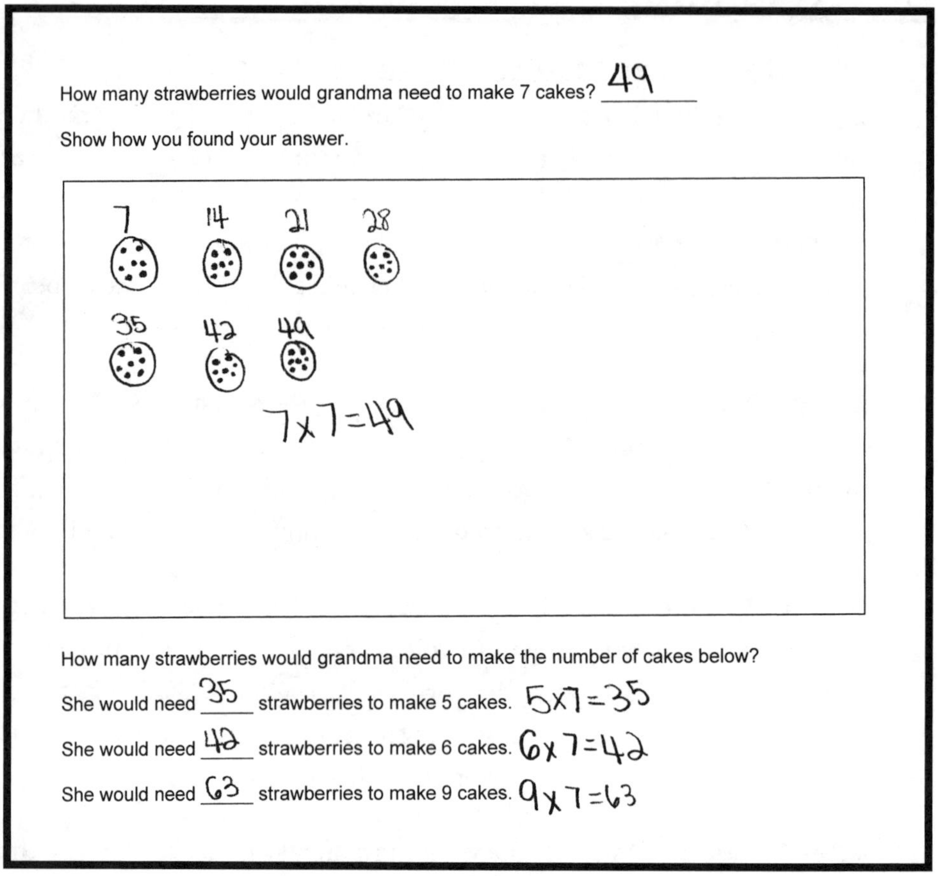
How many strawberries would grandma need to make 7 cakes? 49

Show how you found your answer.

How many strawberries would grandma need to make the number of cakes below?

She would need 35 strawberries to make 5 cakes. 5x7=35

She would need 42 strawberries to make 6 cakes. 6x7=42

She would need 63 strawberries to make 9 cakes. 9x7=63

Ask students how many strawberries Grandma would need for 5 cakes. 6 cakes? 9 cakes? Ask them how they knew the answers. Be sure to highlight the commutative property. Do they know their ×7 facts already?

Exploring the Facts: Square Numbers

Throughout our study of multiplication facts, students have created arrays to display the facts or used centimeter grids to construct area models of the facts. At times, these models create a square, rather than a rectangle. Exploring when squares appear will draw attention to some specific math facts, including the one unknown fact for ×7 facts, 7 × 7.

Have students work with partners to explore square numbers using centimeter grid paper. Can they outline a section to show 2 × 2? Have them record the equation in the outlined section of their grid paper. Challenge them to outline 3 × 3, 4 × 4, 5 × 5, 6 × 6, and so on. Have students observe the area

Figure 12.2 *This student explores square numbers by making area models of math facts.*

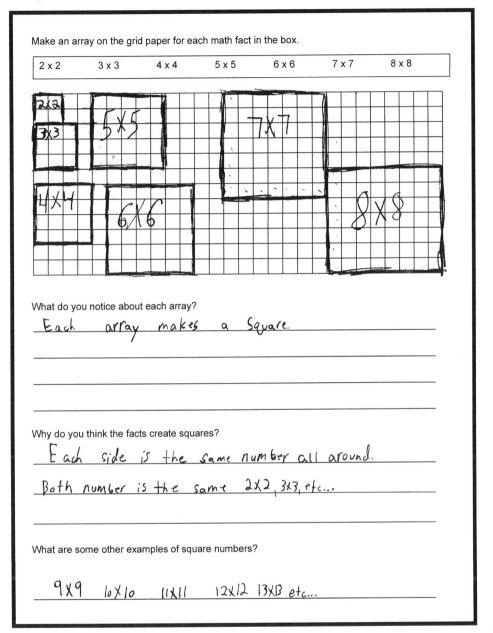

Make an array on the grid paper for each math fact in the box.

| 2 x 2 | 3 x 3 | 4 x 4 | 5 x 5 | 6 x 6 | 7 x 7 | 8 x 8 |

What do you notice about each array?

Each array makes a Square.

Why do you think the facts create squares?

Each side is the same number all around.

Both number is the same 2X2, 3X3, etc...

What are some other examples of square numbers?

9 X 9   10 X 10   11 X 11   12 X 12   13 X 13 etc...

models and share their observations as in Figure 12.2. What do they notice about each outlined area? Why do they create squares? Share the term *square numbers* with students and have them create a list of square number math facts in their math journals. Ask them to explain why these numbers are called square numbers.

Tip To add the excitement of children's literature to your square number investigations, try *Sea Squares* by Joy Hulme (1991) or *My Full Moon Is a Square* by Elinor Pinczes (2002).

Supporting All Learners

Following are additional activities to develop understanding of ×7 facts.

Riddles About Multiples of 7   Riddles challenge students to think about and talk about math facts. Riddles about ×7 facts might include:

> *I am a multiple of 7. I am greater than 20, but less than 40. One of my digits is 5. What am I?*
>
> *I am a multiple of 7. I am greater than 14. My other factor is 3. What am I?*
>
> *I am a multiple of 7. Both of my numbers are even. I am less than 40. What am I?*

Students might write their own riddles about multiplication facts. Riddles can be written on index cards and placed in centers or posed to the class during transition times.

Visualizing ×7 Facts   Provide students with centimeter grid paper (see CD) and ask them to outline areas for the ×7 facts from 1 × 7 to 10 × 7. Have them record the multiplication equations in each outlined section.

Building Automaticity

Although there is only one new ×7 fact, students are likely to still need practice with other ×7 facts to develop automaticity. In addition, this is a great time to engage students in games and interactive activities that review all of the math facts.

Targeted Practice

Spinning Facts   *Spinning Facts* is a great review of the last four fact sets (6–9) and specifically targets the more difficult ×6 to ×9 facts. A student spins a 6–9 spinner twice and then multiplies the two digits to find the product. He covers the product in any one place on his game board (see CD). If the product is already covered everywhere it appears, the player must pass for that turn. Players alternate turns until someone gets three in a row (vertically, horizontally, or diagonally).

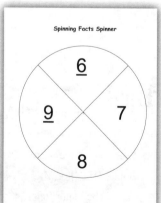

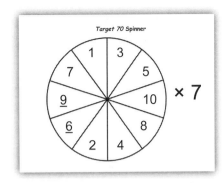

Target 70 In *Target 70* (see CD) players spin and record three products. They then add any two of their three products to get as close to 70 as possible. The player closest to 70 wins the round. The first player to win two rounds wins the game. Like any target game, *Target 70* helps develop problem-solving and estimation skills while practicing math facts.

Family Math Fact Nights Many schools organize family nights during which parents and children engage in math activities. One goal of family nights is to educate parents about productive ways to support their children at home. A Math Fact Night is a perfect way to show parents fun ways to help their children gain automaticity with math facts.

A grade level might collaborate to organize a Math Fact Night, selecting a few math fact games and gathering the materials so parents and students can play them together. Game stations are set up with a teacher or adult volunteer at each station. The teacher or volunteer distributes game materials, explains the game directions, and answers questions as parents and children play together. A rotation signal (a bell or announcement) lets parents and children know when to rotate to the next station.

Have enough materials so parents can take home the supplies needed to play each game. The goal is for parents to learn several games that can be easily played at home, as well as to model a fun and nurturing environment in which students learn math facts in a pressure-free atmosphere.

Tip Modifying Activities to Review Sevens

Modifying fact card activities and math games from previous chapters allows students to practice new facts in a familiar activity context. Adapt one of these for ×7 facts:

Fact Card Arrays (Chapter Four)

Highs and Lows (Chapter Ten)

Sum Up the Facts (Chapter Eleven)

Math Facts Face-Off *Math Facts Face-Off* is similar to the traditional card game of *War*, with one important variation that eliminates the factor of speed. A deck consists of four sets of 0–10 cards (see CD template). The cards are shuffled and dealt to two players. Each player turns over two cards simultaneously. Players find the product of their two cards and state it. The player with the greater product wins that round and gets all four of the cards. Play continues, with players turning over two cards and comparing their products, until one player has all of the cards or time is up. Just like in *War*, if there is a tie (same product), players turn over two more cards and compare, with the winner keeping all of the turned-over cards. In this game there is no speed factor, just lots of practice with math facts! Removing some of the easier factors will ensure lots of practice with the more difficult facts (e.g., four sets of 3–9 cards instead of 0–10 cards).

Tip Substitute a deck of standard playing cards for the four sets of 0–10 cards used in *Math Facts Face-Off.* Simply remove the aces and face cards from the deck. There will be no zeros or ones, so students will get fluency practice with the ×2 to ×10 facts.

Monitoring Progress: Observing Fact Checks

Observing students as they engage in Fact Checks can be very insightful. Which facts are automatic? Which facts slow them down? Which facts bring them to a complete stop? Many teachers carry a clipboard during Fact Checks and discretely jot down observations that might help them identify students who need additional support.

Connecting to Division

As students develop an understanding of multiplication with 7 as a factor, take every opportunity to talk about the connection between multiplication and division facts, and continue to provide students with opportunities to review division facts.

Eliminate Ten

In *Eliminate Ten*, students play with partners or groups and try to be the first player to eliminate all ten cards in front of them. Each player gets a set of 1–10 cards, which are placed faceup in a row in front of them. Each player also has two sets of division fact cards for ×7 facts that result in quotients from 1 to 10 (e.g., $7 \div 7$, $14 \div 7$, $21 \div 7$ …). Players shuffle the two sets of fact cards and then take turns picking one fact card (see Figure 12.3). If they see the quotient in their 1–10 row, they flip it over to eliminate it. The next player then selects a fact card from his deck and eliminates the corresponding quotient from his 1–10 row. The first player to eliminate all ten cards is the winner.

Figure 12.3 *Students work to eliminate all of their quotients in Eliminate Ten.*

Target 7

Target 7 (see CD) is a modification of the multiplication game *Target 70*. In *Target 7*, players spin numbers to find quotients. Students choose two of the three quotients that they spin and add them together to get as close to 7 as possible. The player closest to 7 wins the round. The first player to win two rounds wins the game.

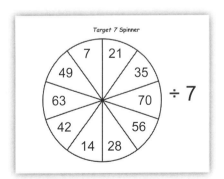

Conclusion

Automaticity with basic math facts provides a solid foundation that supports students as they are continually challenged by the increasing complexity of math skills. But our goals in teaching math facts are much broader than simply providing students with automatic recall of sets of facts. Through explorations with patterns, properties, operations, and number concepts, we focus on building a greater understanding of numbers. To do this, we must rethink the teaching of math facts to include the following principles.

1. The focus of math fact instruction is on understanding numbers and operations. The exploration of patterns and properties helps students make sense of math facts. Big ideas about numbers form the backdrop for math facts instruction.

2. Exploring the meanings of operations is essential before any memorization efforts begin. Connecting math facts to real-world experiences and providing investigations to explore math facts attach meaning to the facts.

3. A teaching sequence that builds on previously learned facts demonstrates the interconnectedness of the facts and supports student learning. Students are able to connect each new set of facts to previous knowledge.

4. Talk and writing during the exploration and practice of math facts help students process ideas and make sense of math facts. Verbalizing observations, making conjectures, justifying solutions, and explaining their thought processes push students to think deeply about numbers.

5. Automaticity takes time. Frequent, varied, and repeated practice moves students toward automaticity. Math facts are not learned through single lessons, but through a series of lessons and practice tasks that are woven together to provide a strong program.

6. Although fluency is a goal, the importance of speed should be minimized to build students' confidence and skills simultaneously. Fluency should be assessed in multiple ways including teacher observation, individual conferences, and Fact Checks.

7. Some students require additional support through small-group or individualized interventions with more and different types of math

fact explorations. Providing additional opportunities for some students to visualize and discuss math facts will support their path toward mastery.

8. Mastery of math facts is only one aspect of mathematical competency. Regardless of where students might be in their pursuit of automaticity, it is important to continue to expose them to a wide range of math skills.

9. The expectations and support of teachers can increase or decrease the anxiety felt by students as they work to master basic facts. Celebration of successes, provision of needed support, connections to prior knowledge, and careful selection of targeted practice activities afford all students a less stressful experience.

Our goal is to build strong mathematicians. Mastery of math facts is an important step toward that goal. If math fact instruction is thoughtful and strategic, it results in more than a student's ability to quickly recall a fact; it cultivates reflective students who have a greater understanding of numbers and a flexibility of thinking that allows them to understand connections between mathematical ideas. It develops the skills and attitudes to tackle the future challenges of mathematics.

References

Professional References

Fosnot, C. T., and M. Dolk. 2001. *Young Mathematicians at Work: Constructing Multiplication and Division.* Portsmouth, NH: Heinemann.

Fuson, K. C. 2003. "Developing Mathematical Power in Whole Number Operations." In *A Research Companion to Principles and Standards for School Mathematics*, eds. Jeremy Kilpatrick, W. Gary Martin, and Deborah Schifter. Reston, VA: National Council of Teachers of Mathematics.

Gravemeijer, K., and F. van Galen. 2003. "Facts and Algorithms as Products of Students' Own Mathematical Activity." In *A Research Companion to Principles and Standards for School Mathematics*, eds. Jeremy Kilpatrick, W. Gary Martin, and Deborah Schifter. Reston, VA: National Council of Teachers of Mathematics.

Marzano, R. J., D. Pickering, and J. E. Pollock. 2001. *Classroom Instruction That Works: Research-Based Strategies for Increasing Student Achievement.* Alexandria, VA: Association for Supervision and Curriculum Development.

National Council of Teachers of Mathematics. 2000. *Principles and Standards for School Mathematics.* Reston, VA: National Council of Teachers of Mathematics.

National Governors Association Center for Best Practices and Council of Chief State School Officers. 2010. *Common Core State Standards for Mathematics.* Available at: www.corestandards.org/assets/CCSSI_Math%20Standards.pdf. Accessed on July 28, 2010.

National Mathematics Advisory Panel. 2008. *Foundations for Success: The Final Report of the National Mathematics Advisory Panel.* Washington, DC: U.S. Department of Education.

Van de Walle, J. 2004. *Elementary and Middle School Mathematics, Teaching Developmentally*, 5th ed. New York: Pearson Education, Inc.

Wiggins, G., and J. McTighe. 1998. *Understanding by Design.* Alexandria, VA: Association for Supervision and Curriculum Development.

Children's Literature

Aker, S. 1990. *What Comes in 2's, 3's, & 4's?* New York: Simon and Schuster, Inc.

Barrett, J. 1978. *Cloudy with a Chance of Meatballs.* New York: Simon and Schuster.

Brenner, M. 2000. *Stacks of Trouble.* New York: The Kane Press.

Buehner, C. 2002. *Snowmen at Night.* New York: Dial Books for Young Readers.

Carle, E. 1977. *The Grouchy Ladybug.* New York: HarperCollins.

Davies, N. 2001. *One Tiny Turtle*. Cambridge, MA: Candlewick Press.

De Rubertis, B. 1999. *Count on Pablo*. New York: The Kane Press.

Geringer, L. 1985. *A Three Hat Day*. New York: HarperCollins.

Giganti P., Jr. 1999. *Each Orange Had Eight Slices*. New York: Greenwillow Books.

Hong, L. T. 1993. *Two of Everything*. Park Ridge, IL: Albert Whitman & Co.

Hulme, J. N. 1991. *Sea Squares*. New York: Hyperion Books for Children.

Hutchins, P. 1986. *The Doorbell Rang*. New York: Greenwillow Books.

Martin, J. B. 1998. *Snowflake Bentley*. New York: Houghton Mifflin Harcourt.

Neuschwander, C. 1998. *Amanda Bean's Amazing Dream*. New York: Scholastic Press.

Pinczes, E. J. 2002. *My Full Moon Is a Square*. Boston: Houghton Mifflin Company.

Polacco, P. 1990. *Thunder Cake*. New York: The Putnam and Grosset Group.

Schwartz, D. 2000. *If You Hopped Like a Frog*. New York: Scholastic.

Sendak, M. 1988. *Where The Wild Things Are*. New York: HarperCollins.

Professional Learning Communities Study Guide

Learning is inherently social. As teachers, it is easy to feel isolated. It becomes especially important that we find opportunities to talk with colleagues and reflect on our teaching practices. Through professional learning communities, we hear new ideas, consider new techniques, clarify our thinking, and ultimately enhance our teaching. It is through conversations with colleagues that we grow as teachers. Teacher study groups value the experience and knowledge of teachers. They provide a forum for rich discussions about teaching and learning. They motivate us to try new approaches and assess our own practices.

Although there are many ways to structure a study group, it is most important to foster a climate in which teachers feel free and safe to participate in the ongoing conversations and exchange of ideas. These study groups should be designed with your teachers in mind. They should focus on the needs of your students and fit the culture of your school. Whether you meet once a week or less often; whether you focus your meetings on a professional book, student work samples, video clips, or a critical question—make the leap into conversation. Here are a few tips to consider as you plan for implementing a study group.

Consider Group Size   Small groups are ideal for study groups, but full-faculty study groups are doable if small-group breakout sessions are an integral part of your planning. You may want to kick off discussion with a general question and then break into smaller groups. Often the optimal number is four to six teachers to ensure there is time for all to exchange ideas. The larger group can reassemble at the end of the session to debrief.

Use Study Questions   Starting with a few questions can jump-start your discussions. There are various ways to use questions.

- Put three or four questions in an envelope and randomly pull them out for discussion.
- Create a chart with two or three starter questions and ask the group to generate more, tapping their own interests and needs.

- Create a list of three or four questions and have teachers prioritize the questions based on the needs of their students.

- Decide on three or four questions and divide the group by interest in the various topics. This allows for a more in-depth study.

- Make copies of the suggested questions for everyone and invite discussion without deciding where to start.

Create an Agenda   Make sure you have planned a beginning and ending time and *always* honor those times. Teachers are busy and knowing there will be a time to start and a time to end is important. Send the agenda to participants prior to the meeting to remind them of the topics to be discussed, as well as any reading to be completed.

Stay Focused on the Topic   State the topic and goals of the session at the start. Plan a procedure that is transparent. You might start by saying something like "Let's decide on a signal to use when we feel the discussion is drifting and then have everyone agree to help stay focused."

Create a List of Norms   Simple expectations that are determined by the group often make study groups function with greater ease and increase potential for success. These can be simple and might include ways to invite a tentative member into the conversation, expectations about listening and sharing, start and stop times, and a procedure for refocusing.

Make It Personal   Make the learning personal for each participant. You might begin each session with teachers turning to a colleague and sharing a quote or teaching idea that resonated with them.

Share Leadership   Rotate group facilitation. Identify several "duties" for the facilitator. Examples might include identifying a question to stimulate discussion, suggesting a big idea from a chapter or group of chapters, posing reflective questions (e.g., "Why do you think the authors kept emphasizing that point?"), and summarizing at the end of the session. Remember that in a study group, *everyone* is a learner. This isn't the place for an "expert"!

Include Everyone   Keep groups small enough so that even the quietest member is encouraged to speak. Active listening on everyone's part will help. Remember that periods of silence should be expected when people are thinking.

Encourage Implementation Decide on an activity or teaching technique that participants will try with students between sessions. Having tried some of the ideas allows teachers to bring insights to the next meeting and ensures that the study group goes beyond talk and into action.

Engage in Reflection Stop from time to time to reflect on what you are learning and how you might make your group's interactions more productive. Make sure you take time to enjoy one another and celebrate your learning.

Set Dates for the Next Meeting Always leave knowing when you will meet again, who will facilitate, and what the general focus will be for the upcoming session.

The following questions relate to the content in each chapter. These are suggestions. Many more concepts and ideas are presented in each chapter. Enjoy!

Guiding Questions

Introduction

1. Why is mastery of math facts important? What problems have you observed when students do not know basic math facts?

2. In what ways would a strong understanding of numbers support students as they focus on math facts?

3. What have you observed about anxiety related to memorizing math facts? Are there types of math fact practice activities that increase anxiety or decrease anxiety?

4. How might attention to the sequence in which facts are introduced support students' mastery of the facts?

Chapter One: Understanding Multiplication and Division

1. What are some misconceptions that might cause early confusion for students just beginning their study of multiplication?

2. What types of models might be used to help students visualize multiplication and division? Why might using a variety of models be helpful for students?

3. What problems might occur if students are asked to memorize math facts too soon?

4. What real-world experiences might make effective multiplication or division problems for students to explore?

Chapter Two: Multiplying by Two

1. What prior knowledge and skills might help students better understand multiplication with two as a factor?

2. What is the role of patterns when multiplying by two?

3. Brainstorm real-world *twos* (e.g., two wheels on a bike) that might provide a context for math facts problems. How will you integrate real-world experiences into your lessons?

4. What types of activities will provide students with ongoing practice with math facts in order to build fluency?

5. How will you know when your students have mastered sets of math facts? How will you determine which students need additional support?

Chapter Three: Multiplying by Ten

1. What prior knowledge and skills might help students better understand multiplication with ten as a factor?

2. What is the role of patterns when multiplying by ten?

3. How might making connections to money concepts enhance students' understanding of ×10 facts? How might you explore these connections?

4. Each chapter presents additional activities to support understanding in the Supporting All Learners section. How will you decide who might benefit from these activities? What will the other students do as you work with small groups of students who need the extra support?

Chapter Four: Multiplying by Five

1. What prior knowledge and skills might help students better understand multiplication with five as a factor?

2. What is the role of patterns when multiplying by five?

3. What are the benefits of incorporating children's literature into math facts lessons? How does a before, during, and after approach enhance the use of children's literature?

4. What types of fact card activities might be effectively used for independent practice or as center tasks?

Chapter Five: Multiplying by One

1. Why is it important to go beyond rules and be sure that students develop an understanding of why the rule is true? How will you do that as you explore the rule for multiplication by one?

2. What is the role of patterns when multiplying by one?

3. Why is it that ×1 facts can be confusing to understand but easy to memorize? What will you do to support understanding?

4. What is the teacher's role during math games?

Chapter Six: Multiplying by Zero

1. Why is it important to go beyond memorizing rules (i.e., "When zero is a factor, the product will be zero.") and be sure that students develop an understanding of why the rule is true? How will you do that?

2. Why is it that zero facts are confusing to understand but easy to memorize?

3. Why might drawing pictures to show zero facts be challenging for students?

4. The first five sets of facts explored within this book (×2, ×10, ×5, ×1, ×0) are called *foundation facts*. What is the significance of these facts? Discuss the difficulty level of the foundation facts in comparison to the remaining sets of facts. Why is this a particularly good time to work on fluency with the foundation facts prior to introducing additional sets of facts?

5. How might you celebrate students' progress toward math fact mastery?

Chapter Seven: Multiplying by Three

1. How might an exploration of the connection between doubles and triples support student understanding?

2. Why are hands-on or visual lessons suggested to develop understanding of math facts? What visuals might be particularly effective for ×3 facts?

3. What are the benefits of asking students to write about their insights after exploring math facts? What types of writing prompts might be especially helpful?

4. What are the advantages of conducting brief, individual conferences to assess math fact mastery? When might you fit conferences into your schedule?

Chapter Eight: Multiplying by Four

1. What prior knowledge and skills might help students better understand multiplication with four as a factor?

2. What is the role of patterns when multiplying by four?

3. What is the significance of the commutative property when teaching basic math facts? How will you continue to reinforce students' understanding of this property?

4. Why is it important that students get opportunities to explore division while they are learning multiplication? How will you promote fluency with division facts?

Chapter Nine: Multiplying by Six

1. What prior knowledge and skills might help students better understand multiplication with six as a factor?

2. Why do the authors consistently suggest partner explorations? What are the advantages and disadvantages of pairing students for math facts explorations? How will you manage partner work so that it is most effective?

3. The authors pose a series of questions about managing math fact games. How would you answer those questions? Record a few ideas for making game time run smoothly.

4. How will you extend learning for students who already know specific math facts? How might you modify games and lessons to provide an additional challenge for students who are ready for it?

Chapter Ten: Multiplying by Nine

1. What prior knowledge and skills might help students better understand multiplication with nine as a factor?

2. How might you support fluency without undue pressure on speed? What are the benefits of students competing against their own past fluency performance rather than competing against the performance of other students?

3. What big ideas should be the focus when learning multiplication with nine as a factor? Why?

4. What are the advantages of modifying familiar math games and fact card activities when addressing a new set of facts?

Chapter Eleven: Multiplying by Eight

1. What prior knowledge and skills might help students better understand multiplication with eight as a factor?

2. How will you relieve anxiety for students who are getting frustrated with memorizing math facts?

3. In what ways do Literature Links enhance math fact instruction? Name some other children's books that would support understanding of a specific set of facts.

4. How will you provide repeated exposure to specific facts for students who struggle with a small group of facts?

Chapter Twelve: Multiplying by Seven

1. Some people view the ×7 facts as the most difficult for students to learn. Do you agree or disagree? Why?

2. How will you identify students who continue to struggle with math facts? What will you do to build their fluency?

3. How will you involve parents in math facts practice? What will they need to understand to best support their children?

4. What planning considerations would make a Family Math Fact Night most effective?

Conclusion

1. What are the most significant ways in which we should rethink the teaching of math facts?

2. The authors contend that automaticity takes time. How do some programs rush students as they learn math facts? How can we ensure that enough time is allowed for students to master facts?

3. Reflect on the teaching sequence of math facts within the book. In what ways might this sequence benefit students?

4. The authors suggest that when taught math facts with a focus on numbers, patterns, and properties, students gain more than automatic recall of the facts. What do they gain from this approach?

5. What tips would you give to a beginning teacher who is deciding how to approach the teaching of math facts?

Additional Study Group Resource

Viewing short video clips of teachers and students in real classroom situations generates discussion, conveys new instructional approaches, and promotes reflection about teaching and learning. For authentic video clips related to math fact teaching, try the following resource:

Bureau of Education and Research. 2009. *Increasing Your Students' Mastery of Multiplication and Division Math Facts.* Bellevue, WA: Bureau of Education and Research.

A Guide to the CD-ROM

The accompanying CD provides you with a multitude of resources that will simplify your planning and reduce your preparation time as you explore math facts with your students. The activities can be used as they appear or can be modified to suit your needs.

Organization of the CD Files

The CD files are organized into four main sections. Each section contains a variety of files to support you as you explore multiplication and division facts.

Teaching Resources

This section holds activities specific to the fact set explored in each chapter. The files are divided into two sections: Featured Resources and Additional Resources. In Featured Resources, you will find all of the recording sheets, game boards, and activity templates that are mentioned within the chapter. For each fact set, Additional Resources have also been provided. These games and activities were introduced in a different chapter for a different fact set but have been modified for the new fact set to provide some additional activity options for students' continued practice.

Teaching Tools

Teaching Tools contains many generic tools that can be used for all fact sets. You will find number cards, number lines, hundred charts, centimeter grids, multiplication charts, and many other tools to support students as they explore math facts.

Fact Cards

Three types of fact cards are provided within this section for each set of math facts. The large fact cards are intended for teacher use. Templates for multiplication and division cards are provided for each fact set. Templates are also provided for small, student-sized fact cards, to allow teachers to easily make sets of fact cards for each student by copying the templates on card stock paper. The final set of fact card templates is for triangle fact cards, to provide a tool to offer combined practice of multiplication and division facts.

Assessment Tools

Several resources are provided to allow you to assess students' mastery of the facts. A Math Fact Automaticity Interview form is included, with directions for conducting student interviews. A Classroom Observation of Automaticity recording sheet, with rubrics, for conducting classroom observations of automaticity is also included. Three types of Fact Checks are included for each fact set: one focuses on the targeted set of multiplication facts, one focuses on both multiplication and division within the targeted fact set, and a third provides a mixed review with current and previously explored facts.

A Fact Check Progress Graph is also included in this section to allow students to graph their own progress. Students shade the bars to show their number of known facts for each try. Although the graph is designed for Fact Checks with twenty-five facts, remember that it can be modified for use with larger or smaller quantities of facts. Simply change the numbers in the left column prior to printing out the graph.

Modifications to CD Activities

The CD holds a wealth of tools and activities that are classroom-ready and aligned with today's math standards. You can simply copy them and begin your lesson. We recognize, however, that our students learn math facts at different rates and struggle with different sets of facts. We know that it is unlikely that one task will provide the right practice for all of our students. A task that is easy for some is simply too difficult for many others. Because these CD files are formatted in Microsoft Word, you are able to quickly modify the activities so they are just right for your students.

If students are struggling with a few specific facts, you might delete some of their known facts from a game and quickly add the ones that they need to practice. If students have already mastered a set of multiplication facts, add complexity to tasks by inserting division facts or more complex multiplication equations. Delete portions of a task if time is a factor, change the writing prompts if you'd like to learn something different about your students' thinking, or separate a task into two parts if you'd like to do some today and follow up with more tomorrow. If your students love a math fact game that was designed for ×4 facts, simply modify it by inserting ×6 facts or ×9 facts and have them play it again and again! This CD gives you the power to design tasks that are just right for your students.

Modifying the CD files is quick and easy. Delete or insert in the same way that you would for any Word document. When you are ready to save your file, simply rename it and save it to your computer or another CD. The original CD will not allow you to save changes directly to it, in order to protect all of the original activities on the CD. Have fun, be creative, and design tasks that are perfect for your students' needs!